Leading Change

"This is a great book. *Leading Change* captures and organizes real-world forces better than anything else I have ever read. I cannot tell you how much I enjoyed it."

Richard A. Guipe, Operations Manager
Tessco Technologies

"An excellent resource for all CEOs trying to orchestrate change throughout their organizations. I intend to share *Leading Change* with my associates, so that together we can gain better insight into the differences between leadership and management and a better appreciation of the magnitude of effort required to lead the transformation process."

Richard Seaman, President and CEO
Seaman Corporation

"A fantastic book that makes a unique contribution to our understanding of change leadership."

David Windom, Chairman
The Windom Company

"Very interesting and relevant, full of practical advice of immediate use."

Richard Deverell, Head of Strategy and Planning
BBC News

"Excellent. I read *Leading Change* last week, and I'm already using some of the ideas in it!"

Kenneth MacKenzie, Chairman
The Mentor I Group, Ltd.

"An exceptional book that I enjoyed reading immensely—Kotter's writing style is excellent. The eight-step change process is a powerful one and deserves substantial critical acclaim in both academic and business circles."

Samuel C. Schwab, President
S. Schwab Company

"I really enjoyed reading *Leading Change*. It is written in a very easy to understand style. I have already shared the book with a number of my key management people, and I am sure our company will benefit if we are all thinking about these issues."

Gerald M. Bedrin, Chief Executive Officer
Allied Strauss Office Products

"Very inspirational."

Steve Guengerich, Managing Director
BSG Corporation

"A fantastic book. The examples of the eight mistakes of managing change as well as the eight-step change process are extremely helpful. By putting the change process in the context of larger social and economic forces, Kotter reframes both previous research on change and his own earlier work."

Rakesh Khurana, Doctoral Candidate
Harvard Business School

"Excellent. I learned a lot from this book and am sure it will be a great success."

John Churchill, Managing Partner
Dunhill Madden Butler

"It is truly imperative for organizations and individuals within organizations to 'lead change'—and that is what this book is all about."

Robert E. Johnston, Jr., Principal
IdeaScope Associates, Inc.

"Unique. Makes many important contributions to our understanding of change leadership in general as well as the details of the process that transforms organizations."

Carl H. Neu, Jr., President
Neu and Company

Leading Change

John P. Kotter

Harvard Business School Press

Boston, Massachusetts

Printed in the United States of America

03 02 01 00   20 19 18 17 16 15

Library of Congress Cataloging-in-Publication Data
Kotter, John P., 1947–
    Leading change / John P. Kotter.
      p.   cm.
    ISBN 0-87584-747-1
    1. Organizational change. 2. Leadership. 3. Industrial
organization. 4. Strategic planning. I. Title.
HD58.8.K65 1996
658.4'06 – – dc20

96-20263
CIP

The paper used in this publication meets the requirements of the American National
Standard for Permanence of Paper for Printed Library Materials Z39.49-1984.

➤ | *Contents*

➤ | *Preface*

In the summer of 1994, I wrote an article for the *Harvard Business Review* entitled "Leading Change: Why Transformation Efforts Fail." It was based on my analysis of dozens of initiatives over the prior fifteen years to produce significant useful change in organizations via restructuring, reengineering, restrategizing, acquisitions, downsizing, quality programs, and cultural renewal. Even as I was finishing that piece I knew I wanted to write more on the subject, so I began this book shortly thereafter.

"Leading Change" was published in the March–April 1995 issue of *HBR*. Almost immediately the article jumped to first place among the thousands of reprints sold by the review, an astonishing event in light of the quality of its large reprint base and of the lengthy time normally required to build reprint volume. Improbable events like this are always difficult to explain, but conversations and correspondence with *HBR* readers suggest that the paper rang two bells loudly. First, managers read the list of mistakes organizations often make when trying to effect real change and said *Yes!* This is why we have achieved less than we had hoped. Second, readers found the eight-stage change framework compelling. It made sense as a roadmap and helped people talk about transformation, change problems, and change strategies.

I've tried to build on both of these virtues in writing this book, and to add a few more. Unlike the article, the book has dozens and dozens of examples of what seems to work and what doesn't. In this sense, it is more hands-on and practical. I've also been more explicit in linking the discussion back to the engine that drives change—leadership—and in showing how a purely managerial mindset inevitably fails, regardless of the quality of people involved. Finally, I've broadened the time span covered, showing how events over the past century have brought us here and exploring implications for the twenty-first century.

Those familiar with my work will see that this volume integrates and extends a number of ideas originally published in *A Force for Change: How Leadership Differs from Management*, *Corporate Culture and Performance*, and *The New Rules: How to Succeed in Today's Post-Corporate World*. Although this book is a logical extension of my past work in terms of subject matter, it is a departure in terms of form. Unlike my previous books, *Leading Change* is not filled with footnotes and endnotes. I have neither drawn examples or major ideas from any published source except my own writing nor tried to cite evidence from other sources to bolster my conclusions. In that sense, this work is more personal than any I've previously published. I'm communicating here what I've seen, heard, and concluded on a set of interrelated topics that appear to be increasingly important.

A number of people have read this book in draft form and offered helpful suggestions. They include Darrell Beck, Mike Beer, Richard Boyatzis, Julie Bradford, Linda Burgess, Gerald Czarnecki, Nancy Dearman, Carol Franco, Alan Frohman, Steve Guengerich, Robert Johnson, Jr., Carl Neu, Jr., Charlie Newton, Barbara Roth, Len Schlesinger, Sam Schwab, Scott Snook, Pat Tod, Gayle Treadwell, Marjorie Williams, and David Windom. A few others have offered much inspiration for the work that underlies this manuscript, especially Ed Schein and Paul Lawrence. My thanks to all.

PART I

The Change Problem and Its Solution

CHAPTER 1

Transforming Organizations: Why Firms Fail

BY ANY OBJECTIVE MEASURE, THE amount of significant, often traumatic, change in organizations has grown tremendously over the past two decades. Although some people predict that most of the reengineering, restrategizing, mergers, downsizing, quality efforts, and cultural renewal projects will soon disappear, I think that is highly unlikely. Powerful macroeconomic forces are at work here, and these forces may grow even stronger over the next few decades. As a result, more and more organizations will be pushed to reduce costs, improve the quality of products and services, locate new opportunities for growth, and increase productivity.

To date, major change efforts have helped some organizations adapt significantly to shifting conditions, have improved the competitive standing of others, and have positioned a few for a far better future. But in too many situations the improvements have been disappointing and the carnage has been appalling, with wasted resources and burned-out, scared, or frustrated employees.

To some degree, the downside of change is inevitable. Whenever human communities are forced to adjust to shifting conditions, pain is ever present. But a significant amount of the waste and anguish we've witnessed in the past decade *is* avoidable. We've made a lot of errors, the most common of which are these.

ERROR #1: ALLOWING TOO MUCH COMPLACENCY

By far the biggest mistake people make when trying to change organizations is to plunge ahead without establishing a high enough sense of urgency in fellow managers and employees. This error is fatal because transformations always fail to achieve their objectives when complacency levels are high.

When Adrien was named head of the specialty chemicals division of a large corporation, he saw lurking on the horizon many problems and opportunities, most of which were the product of the globalization of his industry. As a seasoned and self-confident executive, he worked day and night to launch a dozen new initiatives to build business and margins in an increasingly competitive marketplace. He realized that few others in his organization saw the dangers and possibilities as clearly as he did, but he felt this was not an insurmountable problem. They could be induced, pushed, or replaced.

Two years after his promotion, Adrien watched initiative after initiative sink in a sea of complacency. Regardless of his inducements and threats, the first phase of his new product strategy required so much time to implement that competitor countermoves offset any important benefit. He couldn't secure sufficient corporate funding for his big reengineering project. A reorganization was talked to death by skilled filibusterers on his staff. In frustration, Adrien gave up on his own people and acquired a much smaller firm that was already successfully implementing many of his ideas. Then, in a subtle battle played out over another two years, he watched with amazement and horror as people in his division with little sense of urgency not only ignored all the powerful lessons in the acquisition's recent history but actually stifled the new unit's ability to continue to do what it had been doing so well.

Smart individuals like Adrien fail to create sufficient urgency at the beginning of a business transformation for many different but interrelated reasons. They overestimate how much they can force big changes on an organization. They underestimate how hard it is to drive people out of their comfort zones. They don't recognize how their own actions can inadvertently reinforce the status quo. They lack patience: "Enough with the preliminaries, let's get on with it." They become paralyzed by the downside possibilities associated with reducing complacency: people becoming defensive, morale and short-term results slipping. *Or,* even worse, they confuse urgency with anxiety, and by driving up the latter they push people even deeper into their foxholes and create even more resistance to change.

If complacency were low in most organizations today, this problem would have limited importance. But just the opposite is true. Too much past success, a lack of visible crises, low performance standards, insufficient feedback from external constituencies, and more all add up to: "Yes, we have our problems, but they aren't that terrible and I'm doing my job just fine," or "Sure we have big problems, and they are all over there." Without a sense of urgency, people won't give that extra effort that is often essential. They won't make needed sacrifices. Instead they cling to the status quo and resist initiatives from above. As a result, reengineering bogs down, new strategies fail to be implemented well, acquisitions aren't assimilated properly, downsizings never get at those least necessary expenses, and quality programs become more surface bureaucratic talk than real business substance.

ERROR #2: FAILING TO CREATE A SUFFICIENTLY POWERFUL GUIDING COALITION

Major change is often said to be impossible unless the head of the organization is an active supporter. What I am talking about here goes far beyond that. In successful transformations, the president, division general manager, or department head plus another five, fifteen, or fifty people with a commitment to improved performance pull together as a team. This group rarely includes all of the most senior people because some of them just won't buy in, at least at first. But in the most successful cases, the coalition is always powerful—in terms of formal titles, information and expertise, reputations and relationships, and the capacity for leadership. Individuals alone, no matter how competent or charismatic, never have all the assets needed to overcome tradition and inertia except in very small organizations. Weak committees are usually even less effective.

Efforts that lack a sufficiently powerful guiding coalition can make apparent progress for a while. The organizational structure might be changed, or a reengineering effort might be launched. But sooner or later, countervailing forces undermine the initiatives. In the behind-the-scenes struggle between a single executive or a weak committee and tradition, short-term self-interest, and the like, the latter almost always win. They prevent structural change from producing needed behavior change. They kill reengineering in the form of passive resistance from employees and managers. They turn quality programs into sources of more bureaucracy instead of customer satisfaction.

As director of human resources for a large U.S.-based bank, Claire was well aware that her authority was limited and that she was not in a good position to head initiatives outside the personnel function. Nevertheless, with growing frustration at her firm's inability to respond to new competitive pressures except through layoffs, she accepted an assignment to chair a "quality improvement" task force. The next two years would be the least satisfying in her entire career.

The task force did not include even one of the three key line managers in the firm. After having a hard time scheduling the first meeting—a few committee members complained of being exceptionally busy—she knew she was in trouble. And nothing improved much after that. The task force became a caricature of all bad committees: slow, political, aggravating. Most of the work was done by a small and dedicated subgroup. But other committee members and key line managers developed little interest in or understanding of this group's efforts, and next to none of the recommendations was implemented. The task force limped along for eighteen months and then faded into oblivion.

Failure here is usually associated with underestimating the difficulties in producing change and thus the importance of a strong guiding coalition. Even when complacency is relatively low, firms with little history of transformation or teamwork often undervalue the need for such a team or assume that it can be led by a staff executive from human resources, quality, or strategic planning instead of a key line manager. No matter how capable or dedicated the staff head, guiding coalitions without strong line leadership never seem to achieve the power that is required to overcome what are often massive sources of inertia.

ERROR #3: UNDERESTIMATING THE POWER OF VISION

Urgency and a strong guiding team are necessary but insufficient conditions for major change. Of the remaining elements that are always found in successful transformations, none is more important than a sensible vision.

Vision plays a key role in producing useful change by helping to direct, align, and inspire actions on the part of large numbers of people. Without an appropriate vision, a transformation effort can easily dissolve into a list of confusing, incompatible, and time-consuming projects that go in the wrong direction or nowhere at all. Without a sound vision, the reengineering project in the accounting department, the new 360-degree performance appraisal from human resources, the plant's quality program, and the cultural change effort in the sales force either won't add up in a meaningful way or won't stir up the kind of energy needed to properly implement any of these initiatives.

Sensing the difficulty in producing change, some people try to manipulate events quietly behind the scenes and purposefully avoid any public discussion of future direction. But without a vision to guide decision making, each and every choice employees face can dissolve into an interminable debate. The smallest of decisions can generate heated conflict that saps energy and destroys morale. Insignificant tactical choices can dominate discussions and waste hours of precious time.

In many failed transformations, you find plans and programs trying to play the role of vision. As the so-called quality czar for a communications company, Conrad spent much time and money producing four-inch-thick notebooks that described his change effort in mind-numbing detail. The books spelled out procedures, goals, methods, and deadlines. But nowhere was there a clear and compelling statement of where all this was leading. Not surprisingly, when he passed out hundreds of these notebooks, most of his employees reacted with either confusion or alienation. The big thick books neither rallied them together nor inspired change. In fact, they may have had just the opposite effect.

In unsuccessful transformation efforts, management sometimes does have a sense of direction, but it is too complicated or blurry to be useful. Recently I asked an executive in a midsize British manufacturing firm to describe his vision and received in return a barely comprehensible thirty-minute lecture. He talked about the acquisitions he was hoping to make, a new marketing strategy for one of the products, his definition of "customer first," plans to bring in a new senior-level executive from the outside, reasons for shutting down the office in Dallas, and much more. Buried in all this were the basic elements of a sound direction for the future. But they were buried, deeply.

A useful rule of thumb: Whenever you cannot describe the

vision driving a change initiative in five minutes or less and get a reaction that signifies both understanding and interest, you are in for trouble.

ERROR #4: UNDERCOMMUNICATING THE VISION BY A FACTOR OF 10 (OR 100 OR EVEN 1,000)

Major change is usually impossible unless most employees are willing to help, often to the point of making short-term sacrifices. But people will not make sacrifices, even if they are unhappy with the status quo, unless they think the potential benefits of change are attractive and unless they really believe that a transformation is possible. Without credible communication, and a lot of it, employees' hearts and minds are never captured.

Three patterns of ineffective communication are common, all driven by habits developed in more stable times. In the first, a group actually develops a pretty good transformation vision and then proceeds to sell it by holding only a few meetings or sending out only a few memos. Its members, thus having used only the smallest fraction of the yearly intracompany communication, react with astonishment when people don't seem to understand the new approach. In the second pattern, the head of the organization spends a considerable amount of time making speeches to employee groups, but most of her managers are virtually silent. Here vision captures more of the total yearly communication than in the first case, but the volume is still woefully inadequate. In the third pattern, much more effort goes into newsletters and speeches, but some highly visible individuals still behave in ways that are antithetical to the vision, and the net result is that cynicism among the troops goes up while belief in the new message goes down.

One of the finest CEOs I know admits to failing here in the early 1980s. "At the time," he tells me, "it seemed like we were spending a great deal of effort trying to communicate our ideas.

But a few years later, we could see that the distance we went fell short by miles. Worse yet, we would occasionally make decisions that others saw as inconsistent with our communication. I'm sure that some employees thought we were a bunch of hypocritical jerks."

Communication comes in both words and deeds. The latter is generally the most powerful form. Nothing undermines change more than behavior by important individuals that is inconsistent with the verbal communication. And yet this happens all the time, even in some well-regarded companies.

ERROR #5: PERMITTING OBSTACLES TO BLOCK THE NEW VISION

The implementation of any kind of major change requires action from a large number of people. New initiatives fail far too often when employees, even though they embrace a new vision, feel disempowered by huge obstacles in their paths. Occasionally, the roadblocks are only in people's heads and the challenge is to convince them that no external barriers exist. But in many cases, the blockers are very real.

Sometimes the obstacle is the organizational structure. Narrow job categories can undermine efforts to increase productivity or improve customer service. Compensation or performance-appraisal systems can force people to choose between the new vision and their self-interests. Perhaps worst of all are supervisors who refuse to adapt to new circumstances and who make demands that are inconsistent with the transformation.

One well-placed blocker can stop an entire change effort. Ralph did. His employees at a major financial services company called him "The Rock," a nickname he chose to interpret in a favorable light. Ralph paid lip service to his firm's major change efforts but failed to alter his behavior or to encourage his managers to change. He didn't reward the ideas called for in the change vision. He allowed human resource systems to remain intact even when they were clearly inconsistent with the new ideals. With these actions, Ralph would have been disruptive in any management job. But he wasn't in just any management job. He was the number three executive at his firm.

Ralph acted as he did because he didn't believe his organization needed major change and because he was concerned that he couldn't produce both change and the expected operating results. He got away with this behavior because the company had no history of confronting personnel problems among executives, because some people were afraid of him, and because his CEO was concerned about losing a talented contributor. The net result was disastrous. Lower-level managers concluded that senior management had misled them about their commitment to transformation, cynicism grew, and the whole effort slowed to a crawl.

Whenever smart and well-intentioned people avoid confronting obstacles, they disempower employees and undermine change.

ERROR #6: FAILING TO CREATE SHORT-TERM WINS

Real transformation takes time. Complex efforts to change strategies or restructure businesses risk losing momentum if there are no short-term goals to meet and celebrate. Most people won't go on the long march unless they see compelling evidence within six to eighteen months that the journey is producing expected results. Without short-term wins, too many employees give up or actively join the resistance.

Creating short-term wins is different from hoping for short-term wins. The latter is passive, the former active. In a successful transformation, managers actively look for ways to obtain clear performance improvements, establish goals in the yearly planning system, achieve these objectives, and reward the people involved with recognition, promotions, or money. In change initiatives that fail, systematic effort to guarantee unambiguous wins within six to eighteen months is much less common. Managers either just assume that good things will happen or become so caught up with a grand vision that they don't worry much about the short term.

Nelson was by nature a "big ideas" person. With assistance from two colleagues, he developed a conception for how his inventory control (IC) group could use new technology to radically reduce inventory costs without risking increased stock outages. The three managers plugged away at implementing their vision for a year, then two. By their own standards, they accomplished a great deal: new IC models were developed, new hardware was purchased, new software was written. By the standards of skeptics, especially the divisional controller, who wanted to see a big dip in inventories or some other financial benefit to offset the costs, the managers had produced nothing. When questioned, they explained that big changes require time. The controller accepted that argument for two years and then pulled the plug on the project.

People often complain about being forced to produce short-term wins, but under the right circumstances that kind of pressure can be a useful element in a change process. When it becomes clear that quality programs or cultural change efforts will take a long time, urgency levels usually drop. Commitments to produce short-term wins can help keep complacency down and encourage the detailed analytical thinking that can usefully clarify or revise transformational visions.

In Nelson's case, that pressure could have forced a few money-saving course corrections and speeded up partial implementation of the new inventory control methods. And with a couple of short-term wins, that very useful project would probably have survived and helped the company.

ERROR #7: DECLARING VICTORY TOO SOON

After a few years of hard work, people can be tempted to declare victory in a major change effort with the first major performance improvement. While celebrating a win is fine, any suggestion that the job is mostly done is generally a terrible mistake. Until changes sink down deeply into the culture, which for an entire company can take three to ten years, new approaches are fragile and subject to regression.

In the recent past, I have watched a dozen change efforts operate under the reengineering theme. In all but two cases, victory was declared and the expensive consultants were paid and thanked when the first major project was completed, despite little, if any, evidence that the original goals were accomplished or that the new approaches were being accepted by employees. Within a few years, the useful changes that had been introduced began slowly to disappear. In two of the ten cases, it's hard to find any trace of the reengineering work today.

I recently asked the head of a reengineering-based consulting firm if these instances were unusual. She said: "Not at all, unfortunately. For us, it is enormously frustrating to work for a few years, accomplish something, and then have the effort cut off prematurely. Yet it happens far too often. The time frame in many corporations is too short to finish this kind of work and make it stick."

Over the past few decades, I've seen the same sort of thing happen to quality projects, organization development efforts, and more. Typically, the problems start early in the process: the urgency level is not intense enough, the guiding coalition is not powerful enough, the vision is not clear enough. But the premature victory celebration stops all momentum. And then powerful forces associated with tradition take over.

Ironically, a combination of idealistic change initiators and self-serving change resisters often creates this problem. In their enthusiasm over a clear sign of progress, the initiators go overboard. They are then joined by resisters, who are quick to spot an opportunity to undermine the effort. After the celebration, the resisters point to the victory as a sign that the war is over and the troops should be sent home. Weary troops let themselves be convinced that they won. Once home, foot soldiers are reluctant to return to the front. Soon thereafter, change comes to a halt and irrelevant traditions creep back in.

Declaring victory too soon is like stumbling into a sinkhole on the road to meaningful change. And for a variety of reasons, even smart people don't just stumble into that hole. Sometimes they jump in with both feet.

ERROR #8: NEGLECTING TO ANCHOR CHANGES FIRMLY IN THE CORPORATE CULTURE

In the final analysis, change sticks only when it becomes "the way we do things around here," when it seeps into the very bloodstream of the work unit or corporate body. Until new behaviors are rooted in social norms and shared values, they are always subject to degradation as soon as the pressures associated with a change effort are removed.

Two factors are particularly important in anchoring new approaches in an organization's culture. The first is a conscious attempt to show people how specific behaviors and attitudes have helped improve performance. When people are left on their own to make the connections, as is often the case, they can easily create inaccurate links. Because change occurred during charismatic Coleen's time as department head, many employees linked performance improvements with her flamboyant style instead of the new "customer first" strategy that had in fact made the difference. As a result, the lesson imbedded in the culture was "Value Extroverted Managers" instead of "Love Thy Customer."

Anchoring change also requires that sufficient time be taken to ensure that the next generation of management really does personify the new approach. If promotion criteria are not reshaped, another common error, transformations rarely last. One bad succession decision at the top of an organization can undermine a decade of hard work.

Poor succession decisions at the top of companies are likely when boards of directors are not an integral part of the effort. In three instances I have recently seen, the champions for change were retiring CEOs. Although their successors were not resisters, they were not change leaders either. Because the boards simply did not understand the transformations in any detail, they could not see the problem with their choice of successors. The retiring executive in one case tried unsuccessfully to talk his board into a less seasoned candidate who better personified the company's new ways of working. In the other instances, the executives did not resist the board choices because they felt their transformations could not be undone. But they were wrong. Within just a few years, signs of new and stronger organizations began to disappear at all three companies.

Smart people miss the mark here when they are insensitive to cultural issues. Economically oriented finance people and analytically oriented engineers can find the topic of social norms and values too soft for their tastes. So they ignore culture—at their peril.

THE EIGHT MISTAKES

None of these change errors would be that costly in a slower-moving and less competitive world. Handling new initiatives quickly is not an essential component of success in relatively stable or cartel-like environments. The problem for us today is that stability is no longer the norm. And most experts agree that over the next few decades the business environment will become only more volatile.

Making any of the eight errors common to transformation efforts can have serious consequences (see exhibit 1 on the following page). In slowing down the new initiatives, creating unnecessary resistance, frustrating employees endlessly, and sometimes completely stifling needed change, any of these errors could cause an organization to fail to offer the products or services people want at prices they can afford. Budgets are then squeezed, people are laid off, and those who remain are put under great stress. The impact on families and communities can be devastating. As I write this, the fear factor generated by this

EXHIBIT 1

Eight Errors Common to Organizational Change Efforts and Their Consequences

COMMON ERRORS

➢ Allowing too much complacency
➢ Failing to create a sufficiently powerful guiding coalition
➢ Underestimating the power of vision
➢ Undercommunicating the vision by a factor of 10 (or 100 or even 1,000)
➢ Permitting obstacles to block the new vision
➢ Failing to create short-term wins
➢ Declaring victory too soon
➢ Neglecting to anchor changes firmly in the corporate culture

CONSEQUENCES

➢ New strategies aren't implemented well
➢ Acquisitions don't achieve expected synergies
➢ Reengineering takes too long and costs too much
➢ Downsizing doesn't get costs under control
➢ Quality programs don't deliver hoped-for results

disturbing activity is even finding its way into presidential politics.

These errors are not inevitable. With awareness and skill, they can be avoided or at least greatly mitigated. The key lies in understanding why organizations resist needed change, what exactly is the multistage process that can overcome destructive inertia, and, most of all, how the leadership that is required to drive that process in a socially healthy way means more than good management.

CHAPTER 2

Successful Change and the Force That Drives It

➤ **P**EOPLE WHO HAVE BEEN through difficult, painful, and not very successful change efforts often end up drawing both pessimistic and angry conclusions. They become suspicious of the motives of those pushing for transformation; they worry that major change is not possible without carnage; they fear that the boss is a monster or that much of the management is incompetent. After watching dozens of efforts to enhance organizational performance via restructuring, reengineering, quality programs, mergers and acquisitions, cultural renewal, downsizing, and strategic redirection, I draw a different conclusion. Available evidence shows that most public and private organizations can be significantly improved, at an acceptable cost, but that we often make terrible mistakes when we try because history has simply not prepared us for transformational challenges.

THE GLOBALIZATION OF MARKETS AND COMPETITION

People of my generation or older did not grow up in an era when transformation was common. With less global competition and a slower-moving business environment, the norm back then was stability and the ruling motto was: "If it ain't broke, don't fix it." Change occurred incrementally and infrequently. If you had told a typical group of managers in 1960 that businesspeople today, over the course of eighteen to thirty-six months, would be trying to increase productivity by 20 to 50 percent, improve quality by 30 to 100 percent, and reduce new-product development times by 30 to 80 percent, they would have laughed at you. That magnitude of change in that short a period of time would have been too far removed from their personal experience to be credible.

The challenges we now face are different. A globalized economy is creating both more hazards and more opportunities for everyone, forcing firms to make dramatic improvements not only to compete and prosper but also to merely survive. Globalization, in turn, is being driven by a broad and powerful set of forces associated with technological change, international economic integration, domestic market maturation within the more developed countries, and the collapse of worldwide communism. (See exhibit 1 on the facing page.)

No one is immune to these forces. Even companies that sell only in small geographic regions can feel the impact of globalization. The influence route is sometimes indirect: Toyota beats GM, GM lays off employees, belt-tightening employees demand cheaper services from the corner dry cleaner. In a similar way, school systems, hospitals, charities, and government agencies are being forced to try to improve. The problem is that most managers have no history or legacy to guide them through all this.

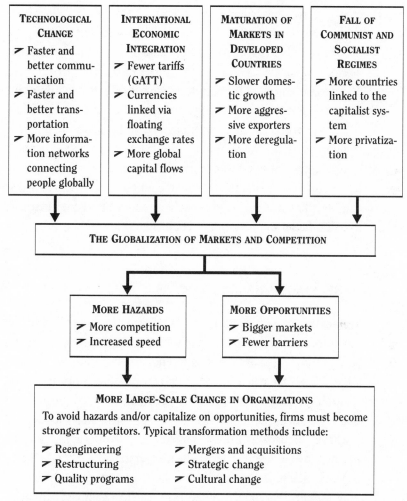

EXHIBIT 1

Economic and Social Forces Driving the Need for Major Change in Organizations

TECHNOLOGICAL CHANGE	INTERNATIONAL ECONOMIC INTEGRATION	MATURATION OF MARKETS IN DEVELOPED COUNTRIES	FALL OF COMMUNIST AND SOCIALIST REGIMES
➤ Faster and better communication	➤ Fewer tariffs (GATT)	➤ Slower domestic growth	➤ More countries linked to the capitalist system
➤ Faster and better transportation	➤ Currencies linked via floating exchange rates	➤ More aggressive exporters	➤ More privatization
➤ More information networks connecting people globally	➤ More global capital flows	➤ More deregulation	

THE GLOBALIZATION OF MARKETS AND COMPETITION

MORE HAZARDS	MORE OPPORTUNITIES
➤ More competition	➤ Bigger markets
➤ Increased speed	➤ Fewer barriers

MORE LARGE-SCALE CHANGE IN ORGANIZATIONS

To avoid hazards and/or capitalize on opportunities, firms must become stronger competitors. Typical transformation methods include:

➤ Reengineering	➤ Mergers and acquisitions
➤ Restructuring	➤ Strategic change
➤ Quality programs	➤ Cultural change

SOURCE: From *The New Rules: How to Succeed in Today's Post-Corporate World* by John P. Kotter. Copyright © 1995 by John P. Kotter. Adapted with permission of The Free Press, a Division of Simon & Schuster.

Given the track record of many companies over the past two decades, some people have concluded that organizations are simply unable to change much and that we must learn to accept that fact. But this assessment cannot account for any of the dramatic transformation success stories from the recent past. Some organizations have discovered how to make new strategies, acquisitions, reengineering, quality programs, and restructuring work wonderfully well for them. They have minimized the change errors described in chapter 1. In the process, they have been saved from bankruptcy, or gone from middle-of-the-pack players to industry leaders, or pulled farther out in front of their closest rivals.

An examination of these success stories reveals two important patterns. First, useful change tends to be associated with a multistep process that creates power and motivation sufficient to overwhelm all the sources of inertia. Second, this process is never employed effectively unless it is driven by high-quality leadership, not just excellent management—an important distinction that will come up repeatedly as we talk about instituting significant organizational change.

THE EIGHT-STAGE CHANGE PROCESS

The methods used in successful transformations are all based on one fundamental insight: that major change will not happen easily for a long list of reasons. Even if an objective observer can clearly see that costs are too high, or products are not good enough, or shifting customer requirements are not being adequately addressed, needed change can still stall because of inwardly focused cultures, paralyzing bureaucracy, parochial politics, a low level of trust, lack of teamwork, arrogant attitudes, a lack of leadership in middle management, and the general human fear of the unknown. To be effective, a method designed to alter strategies, reengineer processes, or improve quality must address these barriers and address them well.

All diagrams tend to oversimplify reality. I therefore offer exhibit 2 on the facing page with some trepidation. It summarizes the steps producing successful change of any magnitude in organizations. The process has eight stages, each of which is associated with one of the eight fundamental errors that undermine transformation efforts. The steps are: establishing a sense

EXHIBIT 2
The Eight-Stage Process of Creating Major Change

1 ESTABLISHING A SENSE OF URGENCY

➤ Examining the market and competitive realities
➤ Identifying and discussing crises, potential crises, or major opportunities

2 CREATING THE GUIDING COALITION

➤ Putting together a group with enough power to lead the change
➤ Getting the group to work together like a team

3 DEVELOPING A VISION AND STRATEGY

➤ Creating a vision to help direct the change effort
➤ Developing strategies for achieving that vision

4 COMMUNICATING THE CHANGE VISION

➤ Using every vehicle possible to constantly communicate the new vision and strategies
➤ Having the guiding coalition role model the behavior expected of employees

5 EMPOWERING BROAD-BASED ACTION

➤ Getting rid of obstacles
➤ Changing systems or structures that undermine the change vision
➤ Encouraging risk taking and nontraditional ideas, activities, and actions

6 GENERATING SHORT-TERM WINS

➤ Planning for visible improvements in performance, or "wins"
➤ Creating those wins
➤ Visibly recognizing and rewarding people who made the wins possible

7 CONSOLIDATING GAINS AND PRODUCING MORE CHANGE

➤ Using increased credibility to change all systems, structures, and policies that don't fit together and don't fit the transformation vision
➤ Hiring, promoting, and developing people who can implement the change vision
➤ Reinvigorating the process with new projects, themes, and change agents

8 ANCHORING NEW APPROACHES IN THE CULTURE

➤ Creating better performance through customer- and productivity-oriented behavior, more and better leadership, and more effective management
➤ Articulating the connections between new behaviors and organizational success
➤ Developing means to ensure leadership development and succession

SOURCE: Adapted from John P. Kotter, "Why Transformation Efforts Fail," *Harvard Business Review* (March–April 1995): 61. Reprinted with permission.

of urgency, creating the guiding coalition, developing a vision and strategy, communicating the change vision, empowering a broad base of people to take action, generating short-term wins, consolidating gains and producing even more change, and institutionalizing new approaches in the culture.

The first four steps in the transformation process help defrost a hardened status quo. If change were easy, you wouldn't need all that effort. Phases five to seven then introduce many new practices. The last stage grounds the changes in the corporate culture and helps make them stick.

People under pressure to show results will often try to skip phases—sometimes quite a few—in a major change effort. A smart and capable executive recently told me that his attempts to introduce a reorganization were being blocked by most of his management team. Our conversation, in short form, was this:

"Do your people believe the status quo is unacceptable?" I asked. "Do they really feel a sense of urgency?"

"Some do. But many probably do not."

"Who is pushing for this change?"

"I suppose it's mostly me," he acknowledged.

"Do you have a compelling vision of the future and strategies for getting there that help explain why this reorganization is necessary?"

"I think so," he said, "although I'm not sure how clear it is."

"Have you ever tried to write down the vision and strategies in summary form on a few pages of paper?"

"Not really."

"Do your managers understand and believe in that vision?"

"I think the three or four key players are on board," he said, then conceded, "but I wouldn't be surprised if many others either don't understand the concept or don't entirely believe in it."

In the language system of the model shown in exhibit 2, this executive had jumped immediately to phase 5 in the transformation process with his idea of a reorganization. But because he mostly skipped the earlier steps, he ran into a wall of resistance.

Had he crammed the new structure down people's throats, which he could have done, they would have found a million clever ways to undermine the kinds of behavioral changes he wanted. He knew this to be true, so he sat in a frustrated stalemate. His story is not unusual.

People often try to transform organizations by undertaking only steps 5, 6, and 7, especially if it appears that a single decision—to reorganize, make an acquisition, or lay people off—will produce most of the needed change. Or they race through steps without ever finishing the job. Or they fail to reinforce earlier stages as they move on, and as a result the sense of urgency dissipates or the guiding coalition breaks up. Truth is, when you neglect any of the warm-up, or defrosting, activities (steps 1 to 4), you rarely establish a solid enough base on which to proceed. And without the follow-through that takes place in step 8, you never get to the finish line and make the changes stick.

THE IMPORTANCE OF SEQUENCE

Successful change of any magnitude goes through all eight stages, usually in the sequence shown in exhibit 2. Although one normally operates in multiple phases at once, skipping even a single step or getting too far ahead without a solid base almost always creates problems.

I recently asked the top twelve officers in a division of a large manufacturing firm to assess where they were in their change process. They judged that they were about 80 percent finished with stage #1, 40 percent with #2, 70 percent with #3, 60 percent with #4, 40 percent with #5, 10 percent with #6, and 5 percent with #7 and #8. They also said that their progress, which had gone well for eighteen months, was now slowing down, leaving them increasingly frustrated. I asked what they thought the problem was. After much discussion, they kept coming back to "corporate headquarters." Key individuals at corporate, including the CEO, were not sufficiently a part of the guiding coalition, which is why the twelve division officers judged that only 40 percent of the work in #2 was done. Because higher-order principles had not been decided, they found it nearly impossible to settle on the more detailed strategies in #3. Their communication of the vision (#4) was being undercut, they believed, by messages from corporate that employees interpreted as being inconsistent with their new direction. In a similar way, empowerment efforts (#5) were being sabotaged. Without a clearer vision, it was hard to target credible short-term wins (#6). By moving on and not sufficiently confronting the stage 2 problem, they made the illusion of progress for a while. But without the solid base, the whole effort eventually began to teeter.

Normally, people skip steps because they are feeling pressures to produce. They also invent new sequences because some seemingly reasonable logic dictates such a choice. After getting well into the urgency phase (#1), all change efforts end up operating in multiple stages at once, but initiating action in any order other than that shown in exhibit 2 on page 21 rarely works well. It doesn't build and develop in a natural way. It comes across as contrived, forced, or mechanistic. It doesn't create the momentum needed to overcome enormously powerful sources of inertia.

PROJECTS WITHIN PROJECTS

Most major change initiatives are made up of a number of smaller projects that also tend to go through the multistep process. So at any one time, you might be halfway through the overall effort, finished with a few of the smaller pieces, and just beginning other projects. The net effect is like wheels within wheels.

A typical example for a medium-to-large telecommunications company: The overall effort, designed to significantly increase the firm's competitive position, took six years. By the third year, the transformation was centered in steps 5, 6, and 7. One relatively small reengineering project was nearing the end of stage 8. A restructuring of corporate staff groups was just beginning, with most of the effort in steps 1 and 2. A quality program was moving along, but behind schedule, while a few small final initiatives hadn't been launched yet. Early results were visible at six to twelve months, but the biggest payoff didn't come until near the end of the overall effort.

When an organization is in a crisis, the first change project within a larger change process is often the save-the-ship or turnaround effort. For six to twenty-four months, people take decisive actions to stop negative cash flow and keep the organization alive. The second change project might be associated with a new strategy or reengineering. That could be followed by major structural and cultural change. Each of these efforts goes through all eight steps in the change sequence, and each plays a role in the overall transformation.

Because we are talking about multiple steps and multiple projects, the end result is often complex, dynamic, messy, and scary. At the beginning, those who attempt to create major change with simple, linear, analytical processes almost always fail. The point is not that analysis is unhelpful. Careful thinking is always essential, but there is a lot more involved here than (a) gathering data, (b) identifying options, (c) analyzing, and (d) choosing.

Q: So why would an intelligent person rely too much on simple, linear, analytical processes?
A: Because he or she has been taught to manage but not to lead.

MANAGEMENT VERSUS LEADERSHIP

Management is a set of processes that can keep a complicated system of people and technology running smoothly. The most important aspects of management include planning, budgeting, organizing, staffing, controlling, and problem solving. Leadership is a set of processes that creates organizations in the first place or adapts them to significantly changing circumstances. Leadership defines what the future should look like, aligns people with that vision, and inspires them to make it happen despite the obstacles (see exhibit 3 on the following page).

EXHIBIT 3
Management versus Leadership

MANAGEMENT	LEADERSHIP
➤ *Planning and budgeting:* establishing detailed steps and timetables for achieving needed results, then allocating the resources necessary to make it happen	➤ *Establishing direction:* developing a vision of the future—often the distant future—and strategies for producing the changes needed to achieve that vision
➤ *Organizing and staffing:* establishing some structure for accomplishing plan requirements, staffing that structure with individuals, delegating responsibility and authority for carrying out the plan, providing policies and procedures to help guide people, and creating methods or systems to monitor implementation	➤ *Aligning people:* communicating direction in words and deeds to all those whose cooperation may be needed so as to influence the creation of teams and coalitions that understand the vision and strategies and that accept their validity
➤ *Controlling and problem solving:* monitoring results, identifying deviations from plan, then planning and organizing to solve these problems	➤ *Motivating and inspiring:* energizing people to overcome major political, bureaucratic, and resource barriers to change by satisfying basic, but often unfulfilled, human needs
➤ Produces a degree of predictability and order and has the potential to consistently produce the short-term results expected by various stakeholders (e.g., for customers, always being on time; for stockholders, being on budget)	➤ Produces change, often to a dramatic degree, and has the potential to produce extremely useful change (e.g., new products that customers want, new approaches to labor relations that help make a firm more competitive)

Source: From *A Force for Change: How Leadership Differs from Management* by John P. Kotter. Copyright © 1990 by John P. Kotter. Adapted with permission of The Free Press, a Division of Simon & Schuster.

This distinction is absolutely crucial for our purposes here: A close look at exhibits 2 and 3 shows that successful transformation is 70 to 90 percent leadership and only 10 to 30 percent management. Yet for historical reasons, many organizations today don't have much leadership. And almost everyone thinks about the problem here as one of *managing* change.

For most of this century, as we created thousands and thousands of large organizations for the first time in human history, we didn't have enough good managers to keep all those bureaucracies functioning. So many companies and universities developed management programs, and hundreds and thousands of people were encouraged to learn management on the job. And they did. But people were taught little about leadership. To some degree, management was emphasized because it's easier to teach than leadership. But even more so, management was the main item on the twentieth-century agenda because that's what was needed. For every entrepreneur or business builder who was a leader, we needed hundreds of managers to run their ever-growing enterprises.

Unfortunately for us today, this emphasis on management has often been institutionalized in corporate cultures that discourage employees from learning how to lead. Ironically, past success is usually the key ingredient in producing this outcome. The syndrome, as I have observed it on many occasions, goes like this: Success creates some degree of market dominance, which in turn produces much growth. After a while, keeping the ever-larger organization under control becomes the primary challenge. So attention turns inward, and managerial competencies are nurtured. With a strong emphasis on management but not leadership, bureaucracy and an inward focus take over. But with continued success, the result mostly of market dominance, the problem often goes unaddressed and an unhealthy arrogance begins to evolve. All of these characteristics then make any transformation effort much more difficult. (See exhibit 4 on the following page.)

Arrogant managers can overevaluate their current performance and competitive position, listen poorly, and learn slowly. Inwardly focused employees can have difficulty seeing the very forces that present threats and opportunities. Bureaucratic cultures can smother those who want to respond to shifting conditions. And the lack of leadership leaves no force inside these organizations to break out of the morass.

EXHIBIT 4

The Creation of an Overmanaged, Underled Corporate Culture

Some combination of visionary entrepreneurship and/or luck creates and implements a successful business strategy.

A fairly dominant position (and thus lack of strong competition) is established in some market or markets—usually a product or service market, perhaps also financial, labor, or supply markets.

The firm experiences much success in terms of growth and profits.

The firm needs, hires, and promotes managers, not leaders, to cope with the growing bureaucracy. Top managers allow these people, not leaders, to become executives. Sometimes top management actively prevents leaders from becoming senior executives.

The pressures on managers come mostly from inside the firm. Building and staffing a bureaucracy that can cope with growth is the biggest challenge. External constituencies are neglected.

Managers begin to believe that they are the best and that their idiosyncratic traditions are superior. They become more and more arrogant. Top management does nothing to stop this trend and often exacerbates it.

A strong and arrogant culture develops.

Managers fail to acknowledge the value of customers and stockholders. They behave in an insular, sometimes political fashion.

Managers fail to acknowledge the value of leadership and the employees at all levels who can provide it. They tend to stifle initiative and innovation. They behave in centralized/bureaucratic ways.

SOURCE: From *Corporate Culture and Performance* by John P. Kotter and James L. Heskett. Copyright © 1992 by Kotter Associates, Inc. and James L. Heskett. Adapted with permission of The Free Press, a Division of Simon & Schuster.

The combination of cultures that resist change and managers who have not been taught how to create change is lethal. The errors described in chapter 1 are almost inevitable under these conditions. Sources of complacency are rarely attacked adequately because urgency is not an issue for people who have been asked all their lives merely to maintain the current system like a softly humming Swiss watch. A powerful enough guiding coalition with sufficient leadership is not created by people who have been taught to think in terms of hierarchy and management. Visions and strategies are not formulated by individuals who have learned only to deal with plans and budgets. Sufficient time and energy are never invested in communicating a new sense of direction to enough people—not surprising in light of a history of simply handing direct reports the latest plan. Structures, systems, lack of training, or supervisors are allowed to disempower employees who want to help implement the vision—predictable, given how little most managers have learned about empowerment. Victory is declared much too soon by people who have been instructed to think in terms of system cycle times: hours, days, or weeks, not years. And new approaches are seldom anchored in the organization's culture by people who have been taught to think in terms of formal structure, not culture. As a result, expensive acquisitions produce none of the hoped-for synergies, dramatic downsizings fail to get costs under control, huge reengineering projects take too long and provide too little benefit, and bold new strategies are never implemented well.

Employees in large, older firms often have difficulty getting a transformation process started because of the lack of leadership coupled with arrogance, insularity, and bureaucracy. In those organizations, where a change program is likely to be overmanaged and underled, there is a lot more pushing than pulling. Someone puts together a plan, hands it to people, and then tries to hold them accountable. Or someone makes a decision and demands that others accept it. The problem with this approach is that it is enormously difficult to enact by sheer force the big changes often needed today to make organizations perform better. Transformation requires sacrifice, dedication, and creativity, none of which usually comes with coercion.

Efforts to effect change that are overmanaged and underled also tend to try to eliminate the inherent messiness of transformations. Eight stages are reduced to three. Seven projects are consolidated into two. Instead of involving hundreds or thousands of people, the initiative is handled mostly by a small group. The net result is almost always very disappointing.

Managing change is important. Without competent management, the transformation process can get out of control. But for most organizations, the much bigger challenge is leading change. Only leadership can blast through the many sources of corporate inertia. Only leadership can motivate the actions needed to alter behavior in any significant way. Only leadership can get change to stick by anchoring it in the very culture of an organization.

As you'll see in the next few chapters, this leadership often begins with just one or two people. But in anything but the very smallest of organizations, that number needs to grow and grow over time. The solution to the change problem is not one larger-than-life individual who charms thousands into being obedient followers. Modern organizations are far too complex to be transformed by a single giant. Many people need to help with the leadership task, not by attempting to imitate the likes of Winston Churchill or Martin Luther King, Jr., but by modestly assisting with the leadership agenda in their spheres of activity.

THE FUTURE

The change problem inside organizations would become less worrisome if the business environment would soon stabilize or at least slow down. But most credible evidence suggests the opposite: that the rate of environmental movement will increase and that the pressures on organizations to transform themselves will grow over the next few decades. If that's the case, the only rational solution is to learn more about what creates successful change and to pass that knowledge on to increasingly larger groups of people.

From what I have seen over the past two decades, helping individuals to better understand transformation has two components, both of which will be addressed in some detail in the remainder of this book. The first relates to the various steps in the multistage process. Most of us still have plenty to learn about what works, what doesn't, what is the natural sequence of events, and where even very capable people have difficulties. The second component is associated with the driving force behind the process: leadership, leadership, and still more leadership.

If you sincerely think that you and other relevant people in your organization already know most of what is necessary to produce needed change and, therefore, are quite logically wondering why you should take the time to read the rest of this book, let me suggest that you consider the following. What do you think we would find if we searched all the documents produced in your organization in the last twelve months while looking for two phrases: "managing change" and "leading change"? We would look at memos, meeting summaries, newsletters, annual reports, project reports, formal plans, etc. Then we would turn the numbers into percentages—X percent of the references are to "managing change" and Y percent to "leading change."

Of course the findings from this exercise could be nothing more than meaningless semantics. But then again, maybe they would accurately reflect the way your organization thinks about change. And maybe that has something to do with how quickly you improve the quality of products or services, increase productivity, lower costs, and innovate.

PART II

The Eight-Stage Process

Establishing a Sense of Urgency

➤ Ask almost anyone over thirty about the difficulty of creating major change in an organization and the answer will probably include the equivalent of "very, very tough." Yet most of us still don't get it. We use the right words, but down deep we underestimate the enormity of the task, especially the first step: establishing a sense of urgency.

Whether taking a firm that is on its knees and restoring it to health, making an average contender the industry leader, or pushing a leader farther out front, the work requires great cooperation, initiative, and willingness to make sacrifices from many people. In an organization with 100 employees, at least two dozen must go far beyond the normal call of duty to produce a significant change. In a firm with 100,000 employees, the same might be required of 15,000 or more.

Establishing a sense of urgency is crucial to gaining needed cooperation. With complacency high, transformations usually go nowhere because few people are even interested in working on the change problem. With urgency low, it's difficult to put together a group with enough power and credibility to guide the effort or to convince key individuals to spend the time necessary to create and communicate a change vision. In those rare circumstances in which a committed group does exist inside a canyon of complacency, its members may be able to identify the general direction for change, to reorganize, and to cut staffing levels. If these executives run a corporation, they might even make an acquisition and put in new compensation systems. But sooner or later, no matter how hard they push, no matter how much they threaten, if many others don't feel the same sense of urgency, the momentum for change will probably die far short of the finish line. People will find a thousand ingenious ways to withhold cooperation from a process that they sincerely think is unnecessary or wrongheaded.

COMPLACENCY: AN EXAMPLE

A major global pharmaceuticals company has had more than its share of challenges over the past few years. Neither sales nor net income growth has kept up with prior hopes or expectations. The firm has gotten bad press, especially after a costly layoff that further eroded morale. The stock is not much higher today than it was six years ago. Complaints about its products are up compared with the mid-1980s, and one important customer has become increasingly negative. A few institutional investors have threatened to dump sizable holdings, an action that might send the stock price down another 5 or even 10 percent. The firm has a proud history and has had significant wins in the past, all of which makes the current situation look rather depressing.

Because the company is in a battle with tough competition, one might expect to find scenes at headquarters that are right out of a WW II vintage film, with war rooms, generals barking orders every two minutes, thousands of troops on twenty-four hour alert, and major assaults being directed on the enemy. But a visit to the company shows nothing of the sort. Visible war rooms don't exist. Generals seem to give orders at a rate that makes baseball look like a fast-paced sport. Many people show no signs of being on alert for eight hours, much less twenty-four. There is little sense of enemy or that the competition is breathing down the company's neck. There is no focus on a compelling mission. Assaults on rivals are often done with BB guns. More powerful shooting with more lethal weapons is aimed inward: workers at managers, managers at workers, sales at manufacturing, ad nauseam.

In one-on-one conversations with employees, everyone readily admits there are problems. Then come the "Buts." But the whole industry is having these problems. But we really are making some progress. But the problem is not here, it's over there in that department. But there is nothing else I can do because of my thickheaded boss.

Visit a typical management meeting at the company and you begin to wonder if all the facts you gathered about the firm's revenues, income, stock price, customer complaints, competitive situation, and morale could have been wrong. In these meetings, reference is rarely made to any indexes of unacceptable performance. The pace is often leisurely. The issues discussed can be of marginal importance. The energy level is rarely high. Discussions become heated only when one manager tries to grab resources from another or to point the finger of blame elsewhere. And most incredibly, every once in a while you hear someone sincerely make a speech about how good things are.

After two days at the firm, you begin to wonder if you've entered the Twilight Zone.

In this complacency-filled organization, change initiatives are dead on arrival. Someone in a meeting suggests that long new-product development cycles are increasingly hurting the firm, but within twenty minutes the discussion has shifted elsewhere and no action is taken to begin shortening development times. Someone else offers a new approach to information technology, yet within a short time the IT group and its ancient system are being praised. Even when the CEO throws out an idea for change, the suggestion tends to sink in the quicksand of complacency.

If you think this story is irrelevant because nothing comparable happens in your organization, I strongly suggest that you look more closely. These conditions can be found almost everywhere. The credit department is a disaster, yet gives no signs of admitting that even a minor problem exists. The French subsidiary is a turnaround case, yet management there seems perfectly content with the current situation.

I cannot count the number of times I have heard an executive claim that all of the people on his or her management team recognize the need for major change only to discover myself that half of that "team" thinks the status quo isn't really so bad. In public, they may parrot the boss's line. In private, I hear a different story. "When the recession ends, we will be in good shape." "As soon as last year's cost-cutting programs kick in, the numbers will go up." And, of course, "The bigger problems are over there; my department is fine."

Q: How big a deal is this sort of complacency?
A: A huge deal.

SOURCES OF COMPLACENCY

Q: So why do people behave this way?
A: For lots and lots and lots of reasons.

When I show twenty-five-year-old MBA students a company that is in trouble yet where complacency is high, they often talk as if the firm were being run by a group of people with an average IQ of forty. Their implicit diagnosis: If the place is in trouble yet urgency is low, then the management must be a bunch of dopes. Their action recommendation: Fire them and hire us.

The MBA student diagnosis linking ineptitude and complacency does not fit well with my experiences. On occasions I've seen inappropriately low senses of urgency among highly intelligent, well-intentioned people. I can still vividly remember sitting in a meeting of a dozen senior managers in a severely underperforming European corporation and listening to an intellectual debate that might have played well at Harvard. And why not? Many of the people around the table that day had degrees from the world's best schools. Unfortunately, both the analysis of alleged competitor mistakes and the rather abstract discussion of "strategy" avoided confronting any of the firm's key problems. Predictably, no decision of any consequence was made at the end of the meeting, since you can't make important decisions without talking about the real issues. I'm sure that the typical person in that room that day was not very happy with the session. These were not fools. But they found the meeting acceptable because on an urgency scale of 0 to 100, the average rating among those executives was certainly less than 50.

At least nine reasons help explain this sort of complacency (see exhibit 1 on the following page). First, no highly visible crisis existed. The firm was not losing money. No one had threatened a big layoff. Bankruptcy was not an issue. Raiders were not knocking at the door. The press was not serving up constantly negative headlines about the firm. As a rational analyst, you could argue that the company was in a crisis because of steadily declining market shares and margins, but that's a different issue. The point here: Employees saw no tornado-like threat, which was one reason their sense of urgency was low.

Second, that meeting was taking place in a room that screamed "Success." The thirty-foot antique mahogany table could have been traded evenly for three new Audis and a Buick. The wall fabrics, wool carpeting, and overall decor were as beautiful as they were expensive. The entire corporate headquarters, especially the executive area, was the same way: marble, rich woods, deep carpets, and oil paintings in abundance. The subliminal message was clear: we are rich, we are winners, we must be doing something right. So relax. Have lunch.

Third, the standards against which these managers measured themselves were far from high. Wandering around that firm, if I

EXHIBIT 1
Sources of Complacency

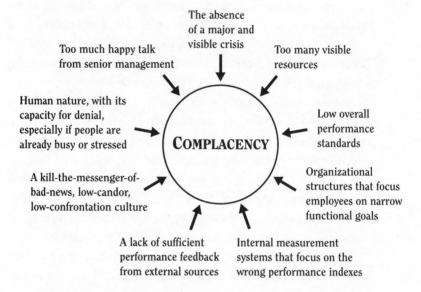

The absence
of a major and
visible crisis

Too much happy talk
from senior management

Too many visible
resources

Human nature, with its
capacity for denial,
especially if people are
already busy or stressed

Low overall
performance
standards

COMPLACENCY

A kill-the-messenger-of-
bad-news, low-candor,
low-confrontation culture

Organizational
structures that focus
employees on narrow
functional goals

A lack of sufficient
performance feedback
from external sources

Internal measurement
systems that focus on the
wrong performance indexes

heard once, I heard ten times: "Profits are up 10 percent over last year." What was not said was that profits were down 30 percent from five years before, and industrywide profits were up nearly 20 percent over the previous twelve months.

Fourth, the organizational structure focused most people's attention on narrow functional goals instead of broad business performance. Marketing had its indexes, manufacturing had a different set, personnel yet another. Only the CEO was responsible for overall sales, net income, and return on equity. So when the most basic measures of corporate performance were going down, virtually no one felt responsible.

Fifth, the various internal planning and control systems were rigged to make it easy for everyone to meet their functional goals. People in the corporate marketing group told me they achieved 94 percent of their objectives during the previous year. A typical goal: "Launch a new ad campaign by June 15." Increasing market share in any of the firm's product lines was not deemed to be an appropriate target.

Sixth, whatever performance feedback people received came almost entirely from these faulty internal systems. Data from external stakeholders rarely went to anyone. The average manager or employee could work for a month and never be confronted with an unsatisfied customer, an angry stockholder, or a frustrated supplier. Some people could probably work from day one until retirement and never hear directly from an unhappy external stakeholder.

Seventh, when enterprising young employees went out of their way to collect external performance feedback, they were often treated like lepers. In that corporate culture, such behavior was seen as inappropriate because it might hurt someone, reduce morale, or lead to arguments (that is, honest discussions).

Eighth, complacency was supported by the very human tendency to deny that which we do not want to hear. Life is usually more pleasurable without problems and more difficult with them. Most of us, most of the time, think we have enough challenges to keep us busy. We are not looking for more work. So when evidence of a big problem appears, if we can get away with ignoring the information, we often will.

Ninth, those who were relatively unaffected by complacency sources 1–8 and thus concerned about the firm's future were often lulled back into a false sense of security by senior management's "happy talk." "Sure, we have challenges, but look at all that we've accomplished." People who were around during the 1960s will remember a terrifying example of this: the many reports of how the United States was winning the war in Vietnam. Although happy talk is sometimes insincere, it is often the product of an arrogant culture that, in turn, is the result of past success.

Much of the problem here is related to historical victories— for the firm as a whole, for departments, and for individuals. Past success provides too many resources, reduces our sense of urgency, and encourages us to turn inward. For individuals, it creates an ego problem; for firms, a cultural problem. Big egos and arrogant cultures reinforce the nine sources of complacency, which, taken together, can keep the urgency rate low even in an organization faced with major challenges and managed by perfectly intelligent and reasonable people.

I think we often assume that if only other individuals were more like us—strong and alert achievers—complacency would not be an issue. Or we think that the people are, for the most part, pretty smart, so all you have to do is give them the facts about poor product quality, sliding financial results, or lack of productivity growth. In both cases, we underestimate the power of the subtle and systemic forces that exist in virtually all organizations. A good rule of thumb in a major change effort is: *Never underestimate the magnitude of the forces that reinforce complacency and that help maintain the status quo.*

PUSHING UP THE URGENCY LEVEL

Increasing urgency demands that you remove sources of complacency or minimize their impact: for instance, eliminating such signs of excess as a big corporate air force; setting higher standards both formally in the planning process and informally in day-to-day interaction; changing internal measurement systems that focus on the wrong indexes; vastly increasing the amount of external performance feedback everyone gets; rewarding both honest talk in meetings and people who are willing to confront problems; and stopping baseless happy talk from the top.

When confronted with an organization that needs renewal, all competent managers take some of these actions. But they often do not go nearly far enough. A panel of customers is brought to the annual management meeting, but no way is found to bring customer complaints to everyone's attention on a weekly or even daily basis. That annual management meeting might be held at a less posh place, but then executives go back to offices that even Louis XIV would not think shabby. One or two relatively frank discussions of problems are initiated at the executive committee level, but the company newspaper is allowed to be full of happy talk.

Creating a strong sense of urgency usually demands bold or

even risky actions that we normally associate with good leadership. A few modest activities, like the customer panel at the annual management meeting, usually fail in the face of the overwhelmingly powerful forces fueling complacency. *Bold* means cleaning up the balance sheet and creating a huge loss for the quarter. Or selling corporate headquarters and moving into a building that looks more like a battle command center. Or telling all your businesses that they have twenty-four months to become first or second in their markets, with the penalty for failure being divestiture or closure. Or making 50 percent of the pay for the top ten officers based on tough product-quality targets for the whole organization. Or hiring consultants to gather and then force discussion of honest information at meetings, even though you know that such a strategy will upset some people greatly. (See exhibit 2 on the following page for nine basic means of raising a sense of urgency.)

We don't see these kinds of bold moves more often because people living in overmanaged and underled cultures are generally taught that such actions are not sensible. If those executives have been associated with an organization for a long time, they might also fear that they will be blamed for creating the very problems they spotlight. It is not a coincidence that transformations often start when a new person is placed in a key role, someone who does not have to defend his or her past actions.

For people who have been raised in a managerial culture where having everything under control was the central value, taking steps to push up the urgency level can be particularly difficult. Bold moves that reduce complacency tend to increase conflict and to create anxiety, at least at first. Real leaders take action because they have confidence that the forces unleashed can be directed to achieve important ends. But for someone who has been rewarded for thirty or forty years for being a cautious manager, initiatives to increase urgency levels often look too risky or just plain foolish.

If top management consists only of cautious managers, no one will push the urgency rate sufficiently high and a major transformation will never succeed. In such cases, boards of directors have a responsibility to find leaders and to place them

EXHIBIT 2
Ways to Raise the Urgency Level

1. Create a crisis by allowing a financial loss, exposing managers to major weaknesses vis-à-vis competitors, or allowing errors to blow up instead of being corrected at the last minute.

2. Eliminate obvious examples of excess (e.g., company-owned country club facilities, a large air force, gourmet executive dining rooms).

3. Set revenue, income, productivity, customer satisfaction, and cycle-time targets so high that they can't be reached by conducting business as usual.

4. Stop measuring subunit performance based only on narrow functional goals. Insist that more people be held accountable for broader measures of business performance.

5. Send more data about customer satisfaction and financial performance to more employees, especially information that demonstrates weaknesses vis-à-vis the competition.

6. Insist that people talk regularly to unsatisfied customers, unhappy suppliers, and disgruntled shareholders.

7. Use consultants and other means to force more relevant data and honest discussion into management meetings.

8. Put more honest discussions of the firm's problems in company newspapers and senior management speeches. Stop senior management "happy talk."

9. Bombard people with information on future opportunities, on the wonderful rewards for capitalizing on those opportunities, and on the organization's current inability to pursue those opportunities.

in key jobs. If they duck that responsibility, as they sometimes do, they are failing to do the board's most essential work.

THE ROLE OF CRISES

Visible crises can be enormously helpful in catching people's attention and pushing up urgency levels. Conducting business as usual is very difficult if the building seems to be on fire. But in an increasingly fast-moving world, waiting for a fire to break out is a dubious strategy. And in addition to catching people's attention, a sudden fire can cause a lot of damage.

Because economic crises are so visible, major change is often said to be impossible until an organization's problems become severe enough to generate significant losses. While this conclusion may be true in cases where a huge and difficult transformation is needed, I think it applies poorly to most situations that need change.

I have seen people successfully initiate restructurings or quality efforts during times when their firms were making record profits. They did so by relentlessly bombarding employees with information about problems (profits up but market share down), potential problems (a new competitor is showing signs of becoming more aggressive), or potential opportunities (through technology or new markets). They did so by setting vastly ambitious goals that disrupted the status quo. They did so by aggressively removing signs of excess, happy talk, misleading information systems, and more. Catching people's attention during good times is far from easy, but it is possible.

One great Japanese entrepreneur regularly stopped his management from becoming complacent despite record earnings by setting outrageous five-year goals. Just when people would start to become smug over their many achievements, he'd say something like: "We should set a target of doubling our revenues within four years." Because of his credibility, his employees couldn't ignore these pronouncements. Because he never pulled the goals out of thin air, but instead put careful thought into what stretch objectives would be feasible given inspired effort, his ideas were always defendable. And in defending them, he tied the objectives back to basic values with which his management identified. The net result: His five-year goals became little bombs that periodically blew up pockets of complacency.

Real leaders often create these sorts of artificial crises rather than waiting for something to happen. Harry, for instance, instead of arguing with his managers' plans, as was normally his style, decided to accept revenue and cost projections that he knew were unrealistic. The resulting 30 percent plunge in expected income caught everyone's attention. In a similar manner, Helen accepted what she believed were unrealistic promises about a major new product introduction and allowed the whole thing to blow up in her face—not an action to be taken by the faint of heart. The result: Business as usual simply couldn't continue.

Some artificial crises rely on large financial losses to wake people up. One CEO of a well-known corporation cleaned up a balance sheet, funded a number of new initiatives, and created a loss of nearly $1 billion in the process. But this was an unusual situation. The CEO had a long-term contract and the firm was awash in cash.

The problem with major financial crises, whether natural or rigged, is that they often drain scarce resources from the firm and thus leave less maneuvering room. After losing a billion or two, you can usually get people's attention, but you end up with far fewer funds to support new initiatives. Even though transformations start more easily with a natural financial crisis, given a choice, it's clearly smarter not to wait for one to happen. Better to create the problem yourself. Better still, if at all possible, help people see the opportunities or the crisislike nature of the situation without inducing crippling losses.

THE ROLE OF MIDDLE AND LOWER-LEVEL MANAGERS

If the target of change is a plant, sales office, or work unit at the bottom of a larger organization, the key players will be those middle or lower-level managers who are in charge of that unit.

They will need to reduce complacency and increase urgency. They will need to create a change coalition, develop a guiding vision, sell that vision to others, etc. If they have sufficient autonomy, they can often do so regardless of what is happening in the rest of the organization. *If* they have enough autonomy.

Without sufficient autonomy in a firm where complacency is rife (not an unusual situation today), a change effort in a small unit can be doomed from the start. Sooner or later the broader forces of inertia will intervene no matter what the lower-level change agents do. Under these circumstances, plunging ahead with a transformation effort can be a terrible mistake. When people realize this fact, they often think they have only one alternative: Sit back and wait for someone at the top to start providing strong leadership. So they do nothing, and in the process strengthen the very forces of inertia that so infuriate them.

Because they have the power, senior executives are usually the key players in reducing the forces of inertia. But not always. Occasionally a brave and competent soul at the middle or lower level in the hierarchy is instrumental in creating the conditions that can support a transformation.

My favorite example is a middle manager in a large travel-related services company who almost singlehandedly confronted top management with data on the firm's increasingly fragile competitive position. She used a nonroutine assignment—to put a product through a new distribution channel—as an excuse to hire consultants. With her behind-the-scenes encouragement, the consultants basically said that the firm would never be able to use the new channel successfully unless it first dealt with a half-dozen fundamental problems. Her peers ran for cover when they saw the results of this work, but she plunged ahead. Because she had political savvy, she deflected most of the criticism created by denial and anger onto the consultants. She had this amazing capacity to serve up lines like: "This really surprised me. Did the consultants screw up or is there something important here?"; "I can't believe that they sent the report to all those people. We didn't authorize that"; "You believe this? So do Gerry and Alice. Have the three of you ever talked about these issues?"

If everyone in senior management is a cautious manager committed to the status quo, a brave revolutionary down below will always fail. But I have never seen an organization in which the entire top management is against change. Even in the worst cases, 20 to 30 percent seem to know that the enterprise isn't living up to its potential, want to do something, but feel blocked. Middle-management initiatives can give these people the opportunity to attack complacency without being seen as poor team players or rabble rousers.

For those in middle management who cannot find a way to help push up the urgency level in a firm that needs change but in which senior management is not providing the necessary leadership, a smart career decision may be to move elsewhere. In today's economic environment, people often cling to their jobs, even if their firms are going nowhere. They convince themselves that with all the downsizing they are lucky to have a paycheck and health-care benefits. This attitude is understandable. But in the world of the twenty-first century, we will all need to learn and grow throughout our careers. One of the many problems in complacent organizations is that rigidity and conservatism make learning difficult.

Punching a time clock, collecting a check, learning little, and allowing the urgency rate to remain low is at best a parochial and short-term strategy. Parochial and short-term strategies rarely lead to long-term success anymore, for either companies or their employees.

How Much Urgency Is Enough?

Regardless of how the process is started or by whom, most firms find it difficult to make much progress in phases 2–4 of a major change effort unless most managers honestly believe that the status quo is unacceptable. Sustaining a transformation effort in stages 7 and 8 demands an even greater commitment. A majority of employees, perhaps 75 percent of management overall, and virtually all of the top executives need to believe that considerable change is absolutely essential.

Because some initial movement is possible with low levels of urgency and because the assault on complacency may create anxiety, it can be tempting to skip stage 1 and begin the transformation process with a later step. I've seen people start by building the change coalition, by creating the change vision, or by simply making changes (reorganizing, laying off staff, making an acquisition). But the problems of inertia and complacency always seem to catch up with them. Sometimes they quickly hit a wall, as when a lack of urgency makes it impossible to put together a powerful enough leadership team to guide the changes. Sometimes people go for years—perhaps with an acquisition fueling growth and excitement—before it becomes apparent that various initiatives are flagging.

Even when people do begin major change efforts with complacency-reduction exercises, they sometimes convince themselves that the job is done when in fact more work is necessary. I have seen exceptionally capable individuals fall into this trap. They speak with fellow executives who only reinforce their rationalizations. "We're all ready for this. Everyone understands that the current situation has to be changed. There's not much complacency around here. Right Phil? Right Carol?" They move ahead on a shaky base and eventually come to regret it.

Outsiders can be helpful here. Ask well-informed customers, suppliers, or stockholders what they think. Is the urgency rate high enough? Is complacency low enough? Don't just talk to fellow employees who have the same incentives as you to discount reality. And don't ask these questions only of a few friends on the outside. Talk to others who know your firm or even to people who seem to be at odds with your organization. And, most important, *muster up the courage to listen carefully.*

If you do this, you will find that some people are not well enough informed to offer a credible judgment and that others have axes to grind. But you can sort all of this out if you talk to enough people. The point is to counteract insider myopia with external data. In a fast-moving world, insider myopia can be deadly.

CHAPTER 4

Creating the Guiding Coalition

MAJOR TRANSFORMATIONS ARE often associated with one highly visible individual. Consider Chrysler's comeback from near bankruptcy in the early 1980s, and we think of Lee Iacocca. Mention Wal-Mart's ascension from small-fry to industry leader, and Sam Walton comes to mind. Read about IBM's efforts to renew itself, and the story centers around Lou Gerstner. After a while, one might easily conclude that the kind of leadership that is so critical to any change can come only from a single larger-than-life person.

This is a very dangerous belief.

Because major change is so difficult to accomplish, a powerful force is required to sustain the process. No one individual, even a monarch-like CEO, is ever able to develop the right vision, communicate it to large numbers of people, eliminate all the key obstacles, generate short-term wins, lead and manage dozens of change projects, and anchor new approaches deep in the organization's culture. Weak committees are even worse. A strong guiding coalition is always needed—one with the right composition, level of trust, and shared objective. Building such a team is always an essential part of the early stages of any effort to restructure, reengineer, or retool a set of strategies.

GOING IT ALONE: THE ISOLATED CEO

The food company in this case had an economic track record between 1975 and 1990 that was extraordinary. Then the industry changed, and the firm stumbled badly.

The CEO was a remarkable individual. Being 20 percent leader, 40 percent manager, and the rest financial genius, he had guided his company successfully by making shrewd acquisitions and running a tight ship. When his industry changed in the late 1980s, he tried to transform the firm to cope with the new conditions. And he did so with the same style he had been using for fifteen years—that of a monarch, with advisors.

"King" Henry had an executive committee, but it was an information-gathering/dispensing group, not a decision-making body. The real work was done outside the meetings. Henry would think about an issue alone in his office. He would then share an idea with Charlotte and listen to her comments. He would have lunch with Frank and ask him a few questions. He would play golf with Ari and note his reaction to an idea. Eventually, the CEO would make a decision by himself. Then, depending on the nature of the decision, he would announce it at an executive committee meeting or, if the matter was somehow sensitive, tell his staff one at a time in his office. They in turn would pass the information on to others as needed.

This process worked remarkably well between 1975 and 1990 for at least four reasons: (1) the pace of change in Henry's markets was not very fast, (2) he knew the industry well, (3) his company had such a strong position that being late or wrong on any one decision was not that risky, and (4) Henry was one smart fellow.

And then the industry changed.

For four years, until his retirement in 1994, Henry tried to lead a transformation effort using the same process that had served him so well for so long. But this time the approach did not work because both the number and the nature of the decisions being made were different in some important ways.

Prior to 1990, the issues were on average smaller, less complex, less emotionally charged, and less numerous. A smart person, using the one-on-one discussion format, could make good decisions and have them implemented. With the industry in flux and the need for major change inside the firm, the issues suddenly came faster and bigger. One person, even an exceptionally capable individual, could no longer handle this decision stream well. Choices were made and communicated too slowly. Choices were made without a full understanding of the issues. Employees were asked to make sacrifices without a clear sense of why they should do so.

After two years, objective evidence suggested that Henry's approach wasn't working. Instead of changing, he became more isolated and pushed harder. One questionable acquisition and a bitter layoff later, he reluctantly retired (with more than a small push from his board).

RUNNING ON EMPTY: THE LOW-CREDIBILITY COMMITTEE

This second scenario I have probably seen two dozen times. The biggest champion of change is the human resource executive, the quality officer, or the head of strategic planning. Someone talks the boss into putting this staff officer in charge of a task force that includes people from a number of departments and an outside consultant or two. The group may include an up-and-coming leader in the organization, but it does not have the top three or four individuals in the executive pecking order. And out of the top fifteen officers, only two to four are members.

Because the group has an enthusiastic head, the task force makes progress for a while. But all of the political animals both on and off this committee figure out quickly that it has little chance of long-term success, and thus limit their assistance, involvement, and commitment. Because everyone on the task force is busy, and because some are not convinced this is the best use of their time, scheduling enough meetings to create a shared diagnosis of the firm's problems and to build trust among the group's members becomes impossible. Nevertheless, the leader of the committee refuses to give up and struggles to make visible progress, often because of an enormous sense of dedication to the firm or its employees.

After a while, the work is done by a subgroup of three or four—mostly the chair, a consultant, and a Young Turk. The rest of the members rubber-stamp the ideas this small group produces, but they neither contribute much nor feel any commitment to the process. Sooner or later the problem becomes visible: when the group can't get a consensus on key recommendations, when its committee recommendations fall on deaf ears, or when it tries to implement an idea and runs into a wall of passive resistance. With much hard work, the committee does make a few contributions, but they come only slowly and incrementally.

A postmortem of the affair shows that the task force never had a chance of becoming a functioning team of powerful people who shared a sense of problems, opportunities, and commitment to change. From the outset, the group never had the credibility necessary to provide strong leadership. Without that credibility, you have the equivalent of an eighteen-wheeler truck being propelled by a lawn mower engine.

Meanwhile, as this approach fails, the company's competitive position gets a little weaker and the industry leader gets a little farther ahead.

KEEPING PACE WITH CHANGE: THE TEAM

The central issue in both of these scenarios that neither firm is taking into account the speed of market and technological change. In a less competitive and slower-moving world, weak committees can help organizations adapt at an acceptable rate. A committee makes recommendations. Key line managers reject most of the ideas. The group offers additional suggestions. The line moves another inch. The committee tries again. When both competition and technological change are limited, this approach can work. But in a faster-moving world, the weak committee always fails.

In a slow-moving world, a lone-ranger boss can make needed changes by talking to Charlotte, then Frank, then Ari and reflecting on what they say. He can go back to each of them for more information. After making a decision, he can communicate it to Charlotte, Frank, and Ari. Information processing is sequential and orderly. As long as the boss is capable and time is available, the process can work well. In a faster-moving world, this ponderous linear activity breaks down. It is too slow. It is not well enough informed with real-time information. And it makes implementation more difficult.

Today's business environment clearly demands a new process of decision making (see exhibit 1 on the following page). In a rapidly moving world, individuals and weak committees rarely have all the information needed to make good nonroutine decisions. Nor do they seem to have the credibility or the time required to convince others to make the personal sacrifices called for in implementing changes. Only teams with the right composition and sufficient trust among members can be highly effective under these new circumstances. This new truism applies equally well to a guiding change coalition on the factory floor, in the new-product development process, or at the very top of an organization during a major transformation effort. A guiding coalition that operates as an effective team can process more information, more quickly. It can also speed the implementation

EXHIBIT 1
Decision Making in Today's Business Environment

TODAY'S BUSINESS ENVIRONMENT

➤ Demands more large-scale change via new strategies, reengineering, restructuring, mergers, acquisitions, downsizing, new product or market development, etc.

↓

DECISIONS MADE INSIDE THE FIRM ARE

➤ Based on bigger, more complex, more emotionally charged issues
➤ Made more quickly
➤ Made in a less certain environment
➤ Require more sacrifice from those implementing the decisions

↓

A NEW DECISION-MAKING PROCESS

➤ Is required because no one individual has the information needed to make all major decisions or the time and credibility needed to convince lots of people to implement the decisions
➤ Must be guided by a powerful coalition that can act as a team

---

of new approaches because powerful people are truly informed and committed to key decisions.

So why don't managers use teams more often to help produce change? To some degree, a conflict of interest is involved. Teams aren't promoted, individuals are, and individuals need unambiguous track records to advance their careers. The argument "I was on a team that . . ." doesn't sell well in most places today.

But to an even greater degree, the problem is related to history. Most senior-level executives were raised managerially in an era when teamwork was not essential. They may have talked "team" and used sports metaphors, but the reality was hierarchical—typically, a boss and his eight direct reports. Having seen many examples of poorly functioning committees, where everything moves slower instead of faster, they are often much more comfortable in sticking with the old format, even if it is working less and less well over time.

The net result: In a lot of reengineering and restrategizing efforts, people simply skip this step or give it minimum attention. They then race ahead to try to create the vision, or downsize the organization, or whatever. But sooner or later, the lack of a strong team to guide the effort proves fatal.

PUTTING TOGETHER THE GUIDING COALITION

The first step in putting together the kind of team that can direct a change effort is to find the right membership. Four key characteristics seem to be essential to effective guiding coalitions. They are:

1. *Position power:* Are enough key players on board, especially the main line managers, so that those left out cannot easily block progress?

2. *Expertise:* Are the various points of view—in terms of discipline, work experience, nationality, etc.—relevant to the task at hand adequately represented so that informed, intelligent decisions will be made?

3. *Credibility:* Does the group have enough people with good reputations in the firm so that its pronouncements will be taken seriously by other employees?

4. *Leadership:* Does the group include enough proven leaders to be able to drive the change process?

This last concern, about leadership, is particularly important. You need both management and leadership skills on the guiding coalition, and they must work in tandem, teamwork style. The former keeps the whole process under control, while the latter drives the change. (The grids in exhibit 2 on the following page depict various combinations of leadership and management that may or may not work.)

EXHIBIT 2
Profiles of Four Different Guiding Coalitions

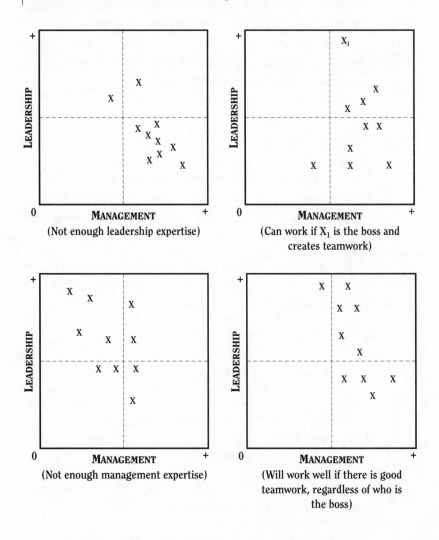

(Not enough leadership expertise)

(Can work if X₁ is the boss and creates teamwork)

(Not enough management expertise)

(Will work well if there is good teamwork, regardless of who is the boss)

A guiding coalition with good managers but poor leaders will not succeed. A managerial mindset will develop plans, not vision; it will vastly undercommunicate the need for and direction of change; and it will control rather than empower people. Yet companies with much historical success are often left with corporate cultures that create just that mindset that rejects both leaders and leadership. Ironically, great success creates a momentum that demands more and more managers to keep the growing enterprise under control while requiring little if any leadership. In such firms, much care needs to be exercised or the guiding coalition will lack this critical element.

Missing leadership is generally addressed in three ways: (1) people are brought in from outside the firm, (2) employees who know how to lead are promoted from within, or (3) employees who hold positions requiring leadership, but who rarely lead, are encouraged to accept the challenge. Whatever the method chosen to get there, the end result—a team with leadership skills—must be the same. Never forget: *A guiding coalition made up only of managers—even superb managers who are wonderful people—will cause major change efforts to fail.*

The size of an effective coalition seems to be related to the size of the organization. Change often starts with just two or three people. The group in successful transformations then grows to half a dozen in relatively small firms or in small units of larger firms. In bigger enterprises, twenty to fifty may eventually need to be signed up.

QUALITIES TO AVOID—OR MANAGE CAREFULLY

Two types of individuals should be avoided at all costs when putting together a guiding coalition. The first have egos that fill up a room, leaving no space for anybody else. The second are what I call snakes, people who create enough mistrust to kill teamwork.

At senior levels in most organizations, people have large egos. But unless they also have a realistic sense of their weaknesses and limitations, unless they can appreciate complementary strengths in others, and unless they can subjugate their immediate interests to some greater goal, they will probably contribute about as much to a guiding coalition as does nuclear waste. If such a person is the central player in the coalition, you can usually kiss teamwork and a dramatic transformation good-bye.

Snakes are equally disastrous, although in a different way. They damage the trust that is always an essential ingredient in teamwork. A snake is an expert at telling Sally something about Fred and Fred something about Sally that undermines Sally and Fred's relationship.

Snakes and big egos can be extremely intelligent, motivated, and productive in certain ways. As such, they can get promoted to senior management positions and be logical candidates for a guiding coalition. Smart change agents seem to be skilled at spotting these people and keeping them off the team. If that's impossible, capable leaders watch and manage these folks very carefully.

Another type of individual to at least be wary of is the reluctant player. In organizations with extremely high urgency rates, getting people to sign on to a change coalition is easy. But since high urgency is rare, more effort is often required, especially for a few key people who have no interest in signing on.

Jerry is an overworked division-level CFO in a major oil company. Conservative by nature, he is more manager than leader and is naturally suspicious of calls for significant change because of the potential disruption and risk. But after having performed well at his corporation for thirty-five years, Jerry is too powerful and too respected to be ignored. Consequently, his division head has devoted hours over a period of two months attempting to convince him that major change is necessary and that Jerry's active involvement is essential. Halfway through the courtship, the CFO still makes excuses, citing his lack of both time and qualifications to help. But persistence pays off, and Jerry eventually signs up.

It can be tempting to write off people like Jerry and try to work around them. But if such individuals are central players with a lot of authority or credibility, this tactic rarely works well. Very often the problem with signing up a Jerry goes back to urgency. He doesn't see the problems and opportunities very clearly, and the same holds for the people with whom he interacts on a daily basis. With complacency high, you'll never convince him to give the time and effort needed to create a winning coalition.

When people like Jerry have the qualities of a snake or big ego, a negotiated resignation or retirement is often the only sensible option. You don't want them on the guiding coalition, but you also can't afford to have them outside the meeting room causing problems. Organizations are often reluctant to confront this issue, usually because these people have either special skills or political support. But the alternative is usually worse—having them undermine a new strategy or a cultural renewal effort.

Afraid to confront the problem, we convince ourselves that Jerry isn't so bad or that we can maneuver around him. So we move on, only to curse ourselves later for not dealing with the issue.

In this kind of situation, remember the following: *Personnel problems that can be ignored during easy times can cause serious trouble in a tougher, faster-moving, globalizing economy.*

BUILDING AN EFFECTIVE TEAM BASED ON TRUST AND A COMMON GOAL

Teamwork on a guiding change coalition can be created in many different ways. But regardless of the process used, one component is necessary: trust. When trust is present, you will usually be able to create teamwork. When it is missing, you won't.

Trust is absent in many organizations. People who have spent their careers in a single department or division are often taught loyalty to their immediate group and distrust of the motives of others, even if they are in the same firm. Lack of communication and many other factors heighten misplaced rivalry. So the engineers view the salespeople with great suspicion, the German subsidiary looks at the American parent with disdain, and so on.

When employees promoted up from these groups are asked to work together on a guiding coalition during a change effort, teamwork rarely comes easily because of the residual lack of trust. The resulting parochial game playing can prevent a needed transformation from taking place.

This single insight about trust can be most helpful in judging whether a particular set of activities will produce the kind of team that is needed. If the activities create the mutual understanding, respect, and caring associated with trust, then you're on the right road. If they don't, you're not.

Forty years ago, firms that tried to build teams used mostly informal social activity. All the executives met one another's families. Over golf, Christmas parties, and dinners, they developed relationships based on mutual understanding and trust.

Family-oriented social activity is still used to build teams, but it has a number of serious drawbacks today. First, it is a slow process. Occasional activity that is not aimed primarily at team building can take a decade or more. Second, it works best in families with only one working spouse. In the world of dual careers, few of us have enough time for frequent social obligations in two different organizations. Third, this kind of group development process tends to exert strong pressures to conform. Political ideas, lifestyles, and hobbies are all pushed toward the mean. Someone who is different has to conform or leave. Groupthink, in the negative sense of the term, can be a consequence.

Team building today usually has to move faster, allow for more diversity, and do without at-home spouses. To accommodate this reality, by far the most common vehicle used now is some form of carefully planned off-site set of meetings. A group of eight or twelve or twenty-four go somewhere for two to five days with the explicit objective of becoming more of a team. They talk, analyze, climb mountains, and play games, all for the purpose of increasing mutual understanding and trust.

The first attempts at this sort of activity, about thirty years ago, were so much like a kind of quick-and-dirty group therapy that they often did not work. More recently, the emphasis has shifted to both more intellectual tasks aimed at the head and bonding activities aimed at the heart. People look long and hard at some data about the industry and then go sailing together.

A typical off-site retreat involves ten to fifty people for three to six days. Internal staff or external consultants help plan the meeting. Much of the time is spent encouraging honest discussions about how individuals think and feel with regard to the organization, its problems and opportunities. Communication channels between people are opened or strengthened. Mutual understanding is enlarged. Intellectual and social activities are designed to encourage the growth of trust.

Such team-building outings much too often still fail to achieve results. Expectations are sometimes set too high for a single three-day event, or the meeting is not planned with enough care or expertise. But the trend is clear. We are getting better at this sort of activity.

For example: Division president Sam Johnson is trying to pull together a group of ten people into an effective change coalition for his consumer electronics business. They include his seven direct reports, the head of the one department in the division that will probably be at the center of the change effort, the executive VP at headquarters, and himself. With great difficulty, he schedules a week-long meeting for all ten of them. They start with a two-day Outward Bound type of activity, in which the group lives together outdoors for forty-eight hours and undertakes strenuous physical tasks like sailing and mountain climbing. During these two days, they get to know one another better and are reminded why teamwork is important. On days three to five, they check into a hotel, are given a great deal of data about the division's competitors and customers, and are asked to produce a series of discussion papers on a tight time schedule. They work from 7:30 A.M. to 7:00 P.M., mostly in ever-shifting, but not randomly chosen, subgroups. From 7:00 to 9:30 each evening they have dinner and talk about their careers, their aspirations, and other more personal topics. In the process, they get to know one another even better and begin to develop shared perspectives on their industry. The increased understanding, the relationships built on actual task achievement, and the common perspectives all foster trust.

Recognizing that this successful week-long activity is just the beginning of a process, Sam hosts another three-day event for the group a few months later. Two years after that, with turnover and promotions changing the makeup of his group, he puts together yet another carefully planned retreat. Just as important, in between these very visible activities, he takes dozens of actions designed to help build the trust necessary for teamwork. Rumors that might erode goodwill are confronted with lightning speed and accurate information. People who know each other least well are put together on other task forces. All ten are included as often as is practical in social activities.

Q: Was this easy to do?
A: Hardly.

Two of the ten in this case were very independent individuals who couldn't fathom why they should all go climb mountains together. One was so busy that scheduling group activities seemed at times an impossibility. One had a borderline big ego problem. Because of past events, two didn't get along well. Yet Sam managed to overcome all of this and develop an effective guiding coalition.

I think he succeeded because he wanted very much for the division to do well, because he was convinced that major change was necessary to make the business a winner, and because he believed that that change couldn't happen without an effective guiding coalition. So in a sense, Sam felt he had no choice. He had to create the trust and teamwork. And he did.

When people fail to develop the coalition needed to guide change, the most common reason is that down deep they really don't think a transformation is necessary or they don't think a strong team is needed to direct the change. Skill at team building is rarely the central problem. When executives truly believe they must create a team-oriented guiding coalition, they always seem to find competent advisors who have the skills. Without that belief, even if they have the ability or good counsel, they don't take needed actions.

Beyond trust, the element crucial to teamwork seems to be a common goal. Only when all the members of a guiding coalition deeply want to achieve the same objective does real teamwork become feasible.

The typical goal that binds individuals together on guiding change coalitions is a commitment to excellence, a real desire to make their organizations perform to the very highest levels possible. Reengineering, acquisitions, and cultural change efforts often fail because that desire is missing. Instead, one finds people committed to their own departments, divisions, friends, or careers.

Trust helps enormously in creating a shared objective. One of the main reasons people are not committed to overall excellence is that they don't really trust other departments, divisions, or even fellow executives. They fear, sometimes quite rationally, that if they obsessively focus their actions on improving customer satisfaction or reducing expenses, other departments won't do their fair share and the personal costs will skyrocket. When trust is raised, creating a common goal becomes much easier. Leadership also helps. Leaders know how to encourage people to transcend short-term parochial interests.

MAKING CHANGE HAPPEN

The combination of trust and a common goal shared by people with the right characteristics can make for a powerful team (see exhibit 3 on the following page). The resulting guiding coalition will have the capacity to make needed change happen despite all the forces of inertia. It will have the potential, at least, to do the hard work involved in creating the necessary vision, communicating the vision widely, empowering a broad base of people to

---

EXHIBIT 3
Building a Coalition That Can Make Change Happen

FIND THE RIGHT PEOPLE

➤ With strong position power, broad expertise, and high credibility

➤ With leadership and management skills, especially the former

CREATE TRUST

➤ Through carefully planned off-site events

➤ With lots of talk and joint activities

DEVELOP A COMMON GOAL

➤ Sensible to the head

➤ Appealing to the heart

---

take action, ensuring credibility, building short-term wins, leading and managing dozens of different change projects, and anchoring the new approaches in the organization's culture.

Again, in a slower-moving, more oligopolistic, less globalized economic environment, all of this effort isn't usually necessary. But the trends are clear. Today, and more so in the immediate future, we will be seeing many additional attempts to transform organizations. Yet without a powerful guiding coalition, change stalls and carnage grows.

CHAPTER 5

Developing a Vision and Strategy

➤ IMAGINE THE FOLLOWING. THREE groups of ten individuals are in a park at lunchtime with a rainstorm threatening. In the first group, someone says: "Get up and follow me." When he starts walking and only a few others join in, he yells to those still seated: "Up, I said, and NOW!" In the second group, someone says: "We're going to have to move. Here's the plan. Each of us stands up and marches in the direction of the apple tree. Please stay at least two feet away from other group members and do not run. Do not leave any personal belongings on the ground here and be sure to stop at the base of the tree. When we are all there . . ." In the third group, someone tells the others: "It's going to rain in a few minutes. Why don't we go over there and sit under that huge apple tree. We'll stay dry, and we can have fresh apples for lunch."

I am sometimes amazed at how many people try to transform organizations using methods that look like the first two scenarios: authoritarian decree and micromanagement. Both approaches have been applied widely in enterprises over the last century, but mostly for maintaining existing systems, not transforming those systems into something better. When the goal is behavior change, unless the boss is extremely powerful, authoritarian decree often works poorly even in simple situations, like the apple tree case. Increasingly, in complex organizations, this approach doesn't work at all. Without the power of kings and queens behind it, authoritarianism is unlikely to break through all the forces of resistance. People will ignore you or pretend to cooperate while doing everything possible to undermine your efforts. Micromanagement tries to get around this problem by specifying what employees should do in detail and then monitoring compliance. This tactic can break through some of the barriers to change, but in an increasingly unacceptable amount of time. Because the creation and communication of detailed plans is deadly slow, the change produced this way tends to be highly incremental. Only the approach used in the third scenario above has the potential to break through all the forces that support the status quo and to encourage the kind of dramatic shifts found in successful transformations. (See exhibit 1 on the facing page.) This approach is based on vision—a central component of all great leadership.

WHY VISION IS ESSENTIAL

Vision refers to a picture of the future with some implicit or explicit commentary on why people should strive to create that future. In a change process, a good vision serves three important purposes. First, by clarifying the general direction for change, by saying the corporate equivalent of "we need to be south of here in a few years instead where we are today," it simplifies hundreds or thousands of more detailed decisions. Second, it motivates people to take action in the right direction, even if the initial

EXHIBIT 1
Breaking through Resistance with Vision

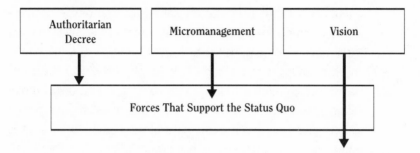

steps are personally painful. Third, it helps coordinate the actions of different people, even thousands and thousands of individuals, in a remarkably fast and efficient way.

Clarifying the direction of change is important because, more often than not, people disagree on direction, or are confused, or wonder whether significant change is really necessary. An effective vision and back-up strategies help resolve these issues. They say: This is how our world is changing, and here are compelling reasons why we should set these goals and pursue these new products (or acquisitions or quality programs) to accomplish the goals. With clarity of direction, the inability to make decisions can disappear. Endless debates about whether to buy this company or to use the money to hire more sales reps, about whether a reorganization is really needed, or about whether international expansion is moving fast enough often evaporate. One simple question—is this in line with the vision?—can help eliminate hours, days, or even months of torturous discussion.

In a similar way, a good vision can help clear the decks of expensive and time-consuming clutter. With clarity of direction, inappropriate projects can be identified and terminated, even if they have political support. The resources thus freed can be put toward the transformation process.

A second essential function vision serves is to facilitate major changes by motivating action that is not necessarily in people's short-term self-interests. The alterations called for in a sensible vision almost always involve some pain. Occasionally, the price of a better future is small; in the apple tree example, all people had to do was sacrifice their comfort for a minute while they walked over to the tree. But in many organizations, employees are increasingly forced out of their comfort zones, made to work with fewer resources, asked to learn new skills and behaviors, and threatened with the possibility of job loss. Under these circumstances, no one should be surprised that a rational human being might view all this without much enthusiasm. A good vision helps to overcome this natural reluctance to do what is (often painfully) necessary by being hopeful and therefore motivating. A good vision acknowledges that sacrifices will be necessary but makes clear that these sacrifices will yield particular benefits and personal satisfactions that are far superior to those available today—or tomorrow—without attempting to change.

Even in situations that require significant downsizing, where the natural inclination is to want to deny the future because it is depressing and demoralizing, the right vision can give people an appealing cause for which to fight. Thus: Our present course will lead us to bankruptcy, but if we go this way we can save some jobs, or prevent problems for our many customers and suppliers, or help the thousands of middle-class families that have invested through their pension funds or other savings in the firm.

Third, vision helps align individuals, thus coordinating the actions of motivated people in a remarkably efficient way. The alternatives—a zillion detailed directives or endless meetings—are much slower and costlier. With clarity of vision, managers and employees can figure out for themselves what to do without constantly checking with a boss or their peers.

This third feature of vision is often enormously important. The coordination costs of change, especially when many people are involved, can be gargantuan. Without a shared sense of direction, interdependent people can end up in constant conflict and nonstop meetings. With a shared vision, they can work with some degree of autonomy and yet not trip over each other.

EXHIBIT 2

71
The Relationship of Vision, Strategies, Plans, and Budgets

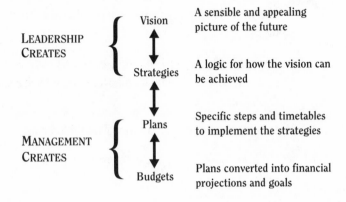

LEADERSHIP
CREATES

Vision — A sensible and appealing picture of the future

Strategies — A logic for how the vision can be achieved

MANAGEMENT
CREATES

Plans — Specific steps and timetables to implement the strategies

Budgets — Plans converted into financial projections and goals

THE NATURE OF AN EFFECTIVE VISION

The word *vision* connotes something grand or mystical, but the direction that guides successful transformations is often simple and mundane, as in: "It's going to pour, let's go under that apple tree for shelter and eat some of the fruit for lunch."

A vision can be mundane and simple, at least partially, because in successful transformations it is only one element in a larger system that also includes strategies, plans, and budgets (see exhibit 2 above). But although it is only one factor in a large system, it is an especially important factor. Without vision, strategy making can be a much more contentious activity and budgeting can dissolve into a mindless exercise of taking last year's numbers and changing them 5 percent one way or the other. Even more so, without a good vision, a clever strategy or a logical plan can rarely inspire the kind of action needed to produce major change.

Whether mundane sounding or not, effective visions seem to have at least six key characteristics (which are summarized in exhibit 3 on the following page). First, they describe some activity or organization as it will be in the future, often the distant

> **EXHIBIT 3**
> *Characteristics of an Effective Vision*
>
> ➤ *Imaginable:* Conveys a picture of what the future will look like
>
> ➤ *Desirable:* Appeals to the long-term interests of employees, customers, stockholders, and others who have a stake in the enterprise
>
> ➤ *Feasible:* Comprises realistic, attainable goals
>
> ➤ *Focused:* Is clear enough to provide guidance in decision making
>
> ➤ *Flexible:* Is general enough to allow individual initiative and alternative responses in light of changing conditions
>
> ➤ *Communicable:* Is easy to communicate; can be successfully explained within five minutes

future. Second, they articulate a set of possibilities that is in the best interests of most people who have a stake in the situation: customers, stockholders, employees. In contrast, poor visions, when followed, tend to ignore the legitimate interests of some groups. Third, effective visions are realistic. They aren't pleasant fantasies that have no chance of realization. Ineffective visions often have a pie-in-the-sky quality. Good visions are also clear enough to motivate action but flexible enough to allow initiative. Bad visions are sometimes too vague, sometimes too specific. Finally, effective visions are easy to communicate. Ineffective visions can be impenetrable.

AN IMAGINABLE PICTURE OF THE FUTURE

What would you think if you saw the following in the company newspaper: "Our vision is to become a firm that pays the very lowest wages possible, charges the highest prices the market will bear, and divides the spoils between stockholders and senior executives, mostly the latter." Stated this bluntly, the message sounds outrageous, yet it is not far from the transformational vision that guides some companies today. Although the cynic in all of us would like us to believe that these firms are doing very well, the truth is that they rarely succeed except for short periods of time, if even that.

Reengineering, restructuring, and other change programs never work well over the long run unless they are guided by visions that appeal to most of the people who have a stake in the enterprise: employees, customers, stockholders, suppliers, communities. A good vision can demand sacrifices from some or all of these groups in order to produce a better future, but it never ignores the legitimate long-term interests of anyone. Visions that try to help some constituencies by trampling on the rights of others tend to be associated with the most nefarious of demigods. Although these kinds of visions can succeed for a while, especially in the hands of a charismatic leader, they ultimately demoralize followers, and they always motivate a counterattack. In business today, these counterattacks come from big institutional stockholders who pressure senior management in a number of ways, from customers who stop buying or join legal suits, and from employees who kill change through passive resistance.

Corporate visions that aren't deeply rooted in the reality of product or service markets are increasingly recipes for disaster. Given a choice—and in most industries today buyers have choices—customers rarely tolerate producers that are not focused on their interests. The same is true in financial or labor markets. If employees or investors have alternatives, the organization that ignores their needs pursues a self-destructive path.

Why would an intelligent group of people pursue a vision that ignores the needs of customers, employees, or investors? From what I've observed, this normally happens when management is feeling pressure from one constituency at the same time that it has a quasi-monopoly position over another constituency. For example: When a strong labor union demands high wages and benefits, a weary management copes by passing all the costs on to customers who have few or no alternatives. Or the reverse: When customers with increasing alternatives from around the world demand better and cheaper products, a beleaguered management copes by squeezing salary and benefits out of weak employee groups. Short-term pressures and the human capacity to rationalize unwise or negative actions can combine to lead reasonable people to act in unreasonable ways.

Asking the following kinds of basic questions can help determine the desirability of a vision for change.

1. If the vision is made real, how will it affect customers? For those who are satisfied today, will this keep them satisfied? For those who are not entirely happy today, will this make them happier? For people who don't buy from us now, will this attract them? In a few years, will we be doing a better job than the competition of offering increasingly superior products and services that serve real customer needs?

2. How will this vision affect stockholders? Will it keep them satisfied? If they are not entirely happy today, will this improve matters? If we are successful in implementing this change, are we likely to provide better financial returns than if we do otherwise?

3. How will this vision affect employees? If they are satisfied today, will this keep them happy? If they are disgruntled, will this help capture their hearts and minds? If we are successful, will we be able to offer better employment opportunities than those firms with whom we compete in labor markets?

Much has been written in the last decade about "balancing" the interests of stakeholders. That's not what I'm talking about here. A vision that balances interests perfectly by promising to provide merely average benefits to customers, employees, and stockholders will not generate the support that is needed to accomplish major change. In competitive customer, financial, and labor markets, more is required. Everyone needs to be served well. Increasingly, the relevant question is not "do we cut costs or improve the product?" but "how do we both reduce our expenses and increase product quality?" Not "do we build a high-ly skilled and well-paid workforce or become the low-cost pro-ducer?" but "how do we create a top-of-the-line workforce that can make us the low-cost producer?"

RETORT: But that's very difficult!
RESPONSE: You bet! And being able to deal with that challenge is more and more what separates winners from losers.

STRATEGIC FEASIBILITY

One sometimes sees corporate visions these days that promise the world but don't provide a clue as to how or why a transfor-mation is feasible. We will go from the lowest in productivity in our industry to the head of the pack. Terrific, but how? We will change from being a middle-of-the-road company to being the customer's preferred choice. Wonderful, but how?

A vision with feasibility is more than a pipe dream. An effec-tive description of the future involves stretching resources and capabilities. A vision that requires only a 3 percent improvement per year will never force the fundamental rethinking and change that are so often needed in rapidly shifting environments. But if transformation goals seem impossible, they will lack credibility and thus fail to motivate action. How much of a stretch will seem feasible is to a great degree a function of the communica-tion process. Great leaders know how to make ambitious goals look doable—and I'll have more to say about that in the next chapter.

Feasibility also means that a vision is grounded in a clear and rational understanding of the organization, its market environ-ment, and competitive trends. This is where strategy plays an important role. Strategy provides both a logic and a first level of detail to show how a vision can be accomplished. For example, because the single biggest trend today is toward faster-moving and more competitive market environments, many firms need to become less inwardly focused, centralized, hierarchical, slow in decision making, and political if they are to succeed in the marketplace, provide superior financial returns, etc. An effective vision and the strategies that back it up must rationally address these realities.

An entire industry has blossomed, mostly in the last two decades, to help organizations with these issues. Strategy consultants gather all kinds of data, especially about markets and competition, and assist firms in making fundamental choices about what products to manufacture and how best to produce those offerings. The huge growth in this kind of consulting business says something significant about the difficulty organizations have in abandoning historical biases, developing new strategies, and assessing their feasibility.

FOCUS, FLEXIBILITY, AND EASE OF COMMUNICATION

Effective visions are always focused enough to guide employees—to convey which actions are important and which are out of bounds. Statements of direction so vague that people can't relate to them are not helpful. Thus, "To be a great company" does not express a very good vision, nor does the slightly more specific "To become the best firm in the telecommunications industry." In both cases, the question left unanswered is "best at *what?*" Having the best cafeteria food? The best parking lots?

Of course, people sometimes go too far in trying to be clear. Effective visions are open ended enough to allow for individual initiative and for changing conditions. Long and detailed pronouncements not only can feel like straitjackets but can soon become obsolete in a rapidly changing world. At the same time, visions that need constant readjustments lose their credibility.

Between the two extremes of impossibly vague and meticulously detailed is a lot of room. In selecting where to operate, executives guiding successful transformations often choose communicability as a key criterion. Even a desirable, focused, and feasible description of the future is useless if it is so complex that communicating it to large numbers of people is impossible.

The point here is not to take a good idea and "dumb it down." But as we will see in the next chapter, communicating even a simple vision to a large number of people can be enormously difficult. Simplicity is essential.

EFFECTIVE AND INEFFECTIVE VISIONS: A FEW EXAMPLES

In some ways, it's easier to describe visions that don't help produce needed change than those that do. For example:

1. "Fifteen percent earnings per share growth" is not an effective vision. As I've seen in a number of companies, such a financial goal will not feel desirable to some, may not seem feasible to others, and offers few clues as to what actions are needed to achieve it.

2. An effective vision is not a four-inch-thick notebook describing the "Quality Program." After reading 800 pages, most people tend to become depressed instead of motivated.

3. An effective vision is not a hopelessly vague listing of positive values ("We stand for integrity, safe products, a clean environment, good employee relations, etc."). Such lists never provide clear direction and turn off everyone but extreme idealists.

So what *is* an effective vision? The management in one U.S. insurance company believes the following is helping to transform the firm:

It is our goal to become the world leader in our industry within ten years. As we use this term, *leadership* means more revenue, more profit, more innovation that serves our customers' needs, and a more attractive place to work than any other competitor. Achieving this ambitious objective will probably require double-digit revenue and profit growth each year. It will surely require that we become less U.S. oriented, more externally focused, considerably less bureaucratic, and more of a service instead of a product company. We sincerely believe that if we work together we can achieve this change, and in the process create a firm that will be admired by our stockholders, customers, employees, and communities.

Statements as brief as this one are sometimes nothing but meaningless happy talk. But read the above paragraph again and you will see that it contains a lot of information. While the statement does not give anything close to a detailed directive, it does provide focus by (1) eliminating many possibilities (for example, becoming a conglomerate, remaining strictly a U.S.-based company, exploiting the workforce), (2) pointing specifically to areas that need to change (for example, from a product orientation to a service culture), and (3) stating a clear target (number one in the industry in ten years). There is an explicit statement about desirability ("admired by stockholders . . ."). And it is reasonably easy to communicate (only a hundred or so words).

An expanded version of this short statement fills three pages and more directly addresses the feasibility issue with a discussion of strategy. But even the content of the three-page document can be conveyed within five minutes. Remember my rule of thumb: *If you cannot describe your vision to someone in five minutes and get their interest, you have more work to do in this phase of a transformation process.*

Here's another example, this one more narrowly focused on a particular project:

The vision driving our department's reengineering effort is simple. We want to reduce our costs by at least 30 percent and increase the speed with which we can respond to customers by at least 40 percent. These are stretch goals, but we know based on the pilot project in Austin that they are achievable if we all work together. When this is completed, in approximately three years, we will have leapfrogged our biggest competitors and achieved all the associated benefits: better satisfied customers, increased revenue growth, more job security, and the enormous pride that comes from great accomplishments.

Like these two examples, the most effective transformational visions I've seen in the past few years all seem to share the following characteristics:

1. They are ambitious enough to force people out of comfortable routines. Becoming 5 percent better is not the goal; becoming the best at something is often the goal.

2. They aim in a general way at providing better and better products or services at lower and lower costs, thus appealing greatly to customers and stockholders.

3. They take advantage of fundamental trends, especially globalization and new technology.

4. They make no attempt to exploit anyone and thus have a certain moral power.

CREATING THE VISION

Over the past decade, I've closely observed a dozen companies as they tried to create effective visions for change. From that experience, I conclude the following: developing a good vision is an exercise of both the head and the heart, it takes some time, it always involves a group of people, and it is tough to do well.

The first draft often comes from a single individual. Such a person draws on his or her experiences and values to create a set of ideas that both makes sense and is personally exciting. In successful transformations, these ideas are then discussed at length with the guiding coalition. The discussion almost always modifies the original ideas by eliminating one element, adding others, and/or clarifying the statement. I have seen some people try to accomplish this in a process that is as disciplined as the formal planning system, but that never seems to work well. Vision creation is almost always a messy, difficult, and sometimes emotionally charged exercise.

In one typical case, the head of a medium-size retail business had his human resources and strategic planning vice presidents draft a statement based on his ideas. That document became the focus of attention at a stressful two-day off-site management meeting. Halfway through that session, despite a beautiful and sunny resort setting, most of the attendees probably wished they were back home in two feet of snow. The boss may even have felt that way himself. The problem was that the draft vision statement brought to the surface a number of conflicting worldviews held by members of the executive committee. It also made one person extremely anxious, because it spoke of a future in which his group would become less important. And for at least two of the attendees, maybe more, the process was too fuzzy and soft. Today, I think almost all the senior managers at this company would agree on the value of that meeting and subsequent discussions. But at the time, the session was not much fun.

Instead of backing down when the conflicts emerged, the boss gently but firmly pushed ahead. He used his not inconsiderable interpersonal skills to keep the pressure at a tolerable level. If he had skipped the first two phases of the transformation process, the meeting might have blown up. But having developed a sense of urgency and established a healthy degree of trust and a shared commitment to excellence, the group was able to work its way through a difficult set of topics and tentatively agree on a modified version of the document.

With notes from that session and some additional staff work, the boss then drafted a second statement, which was discussed with his guiding coalition over a six-month period. He went public with a revised document after that and has added to or modified it slightly on two occasions over the past four years.

Vision creation can be difficult for at least five reasons (as summarized in exhibit 4 on the facing page). First, we have raised a number of generations of very talented people to be managers, not leaders or leader/managers, and vision is not a component of effective management. The managerial equivalent to vision creation is planning. Ask a good manager what his or her vision is, and you'll likely hear about the operating plan— for example, to introduce this product in June, to hire X new people by September, to make $Y after taxes this year. But a plan

---

EXHIBIT 4
Creating an Effective Vision

➤ *First draft:* The process often starts with an initial statement from a single individual, reflecting both his or her dreams and real marketplace needs.

➤ *Role of the guiding coalition:* The first draft is always modeled over time by the guiding coalition or an even larger group of people.

➤ *Importance of teamwork:* The group process never works well without a minimum of effective teamwork.

➤ *Role of the head and the heart:* Both analytical thinking and a lot of dreaming are essential throughout the activity.

➤ *Messiness of the process:* Vision creation is usually a process of two steps forward and one back, movement to the left and then to the right.

➤ *Time frame:* Vision is never created in a single meeting. The activity takes months, sometimes years.

➤ *End product:* The process results in a direction for the future that is desirable, feasible, focused, flexible, and is conveyable in five minutes or less.

---

can never direct, align, and inspire action the way vision can, and it is therefore not sufficient during transformation. In a slower-moving past, we didn't need to teach people much about this sort of activity, so we didn't. Again, history is working against us.

Second, although a good vision has a certain elegant simplicity, the data and the syntheses required to produce it are usually anything but simple. A ten-foot stack of paperwork, reports, financials, and statistics are sometimes needed to help produce a one-page statement of future direction. And the analysis of all that information is not the sort of activity that can be delegated to a supercomputer.

Third, both head and heart are required in this exercise. After seventeen or more years of formal education, most of us know something about using our heads but little about using our hearts. Yet all effective visions seem to be grounded in sensible values as well as analytically sound thinking, and the values have to be ones that resonate deeply with the executives on the guiding coalition. As a result, creating a vision is not just a strategy exercise in assessing environmental opportunities and organizational capabilities. The process very much involves getting in touch with ourselves—who we are and what we care about. In a personal sense, the exercise can be quite rewarding. But for people who are not introspective or self-aware, this activity can also be difficult and anxiety producing.

Fourth, if teamwork does not exist in the guiding coalition, parochialism can turn vision creation into an endless negotiation. I once watched a frustrated group of executives in a computer company work for two years to try to get agreement on the basic elements of a transformational vision. The time spent in formal meetings and in more informal, one-on-one discussions added up to a staggering number of hours. Yet these executives never achieved their objective: the creation of a sensible vision to which they were committed. The biggest problem was that too few people were actually trying to achieve that goal. Instead, most were protecting their subgroup's narrowly defined interests.

Finally, if the urgency rate is not high enough, you will never find enough time to complete the process. Meetings become hard to schedule. Work in between sessions moves slowly. Before you know it, a year has gone by and little has been accomplished. Pressures build to create *something*, so a far less than ideal product is accepted and you move on. Under these circumstances, the resulting vision is usually a small increment from the status quo or a bolder statement that most people on the guiding coalition don't really believe. The fact that the vision isn't quite right, or isn't ambitious enough, or has limited support eventually undermines the change effort.

Because of the anxieties and conflicts attending vision creation, I often see people cutting the process off prematurely. Long before the members of the guiding coalition have had sufficient chance to think, feel, argue, and reflect, the vision is engraved on wall plaques or encased in clear plastic. When this happens, the transformation process is always hurt.

Remember: An ineffective vision may be worse than no vision at all. Pursuit of a poorly developed vision can sometimes send people off a cliff. And lip service without commitment creates a sort of dangerous illusion. People will think they are building on a solid base, only to find that the bottom of the structure eventually collapses, destroying all their work. In either case, once they learn of the problems caused by the premature shutting off of the vision creation process, employees can become deeply cynical about transformation. With deeply cynical people, you rarely achieve successful change.

I've said it before, but the idea deserves repeating. Whenever you leave one of the steps in the eight-stage change process without finishing the work, you usually pay a big price later on. Without a sufficiently strong foundation, the redirection collapses at some point, forcing you to go back and rebuild. For stage 3, creating a vision and strategy, this means taking the time to do the process correctly. Think of it as an investment, an important investment, in creating a better future.

Communicating
the Change Vision

➤ A GREAT VISION CAN SERVE A
useful purpose even if it is understood by just a few key people. But
the real power of a vision is
unleashed only when most of
those involved in an enterprise or
activity have a common understanding of its goals and direction. That shared sense of a desirable future can help motivate and
coordinate the kinds of actions
that create transformations.

Gaining understanding and
commitment to a new direction is
never an easy task, especially in
large enterprises. Smart people
make mistakes here all the time,
and outright failure is not uncommon, even in well-known firms.
Managers undercommunicate,
and often not by a small amount.
Or they inadvertently send inconsistent messages. In either case,
the net result is the same: a
stalled transformation.

Two Cases of Failure to Communicate

A division-level general manager running a telecommunications business says that a group developed a vision for change last year and spent a great deal of time communicating it broadly. Go down a few levels in the hierarchy, and people say, "Vision? What vision?" Checking further, you find that the seeming inconsistency is quite explainable. Senior managers did expend what seemed to them like a lot of effort communicating the vision. They devoted precious time at the annual strategic planning meeting to that topic. They ran three or four articles in the company newspaper. One senior manager spent hours helping to produce a video for employees. And the general subject was on the executive committee agenda during at least a dozen meetings. Furthermore, if you push first-line managers a little harder, they admit to having heard something. But they honestly cannot remember much, mostly because they are overwhelmed with information, only a small fraction of which has to do with the new vision. "Something about customers and partnerships, wasn't it?" And the more candid among them will say: "It was just a bunch of jaw movements. Two weeks after they announced the new vision, they promoted some jerk whose approach is totally inconsistent with that message."

Another disastrous but not uncommon scenario: The vision is communicated often, but poorly. "Our goal is to become the first truly transnational firm at the conjunction of the converging communication/information industries to achieve both a boundaryless organization and a paradigm shift strategy." As ridiculous as this may sound, some interesting ideas lurk in that sentence. But as communication, even if repeated often, the statement works very poorly.

Why does this happen? Failure in the first three phases of a transformation effort often contributes to problems here. When the urgency rate isn't high enough, people don't listen carefully to information about a new vision. If the guiding coalition isn't the right group, it will have difficulty both creating and sending an appropriate message. If the vision itself is too blurry or just a bad idea, selling poor goods becomes a tough job. But even when the first three phases of change are handled well, people still often have difficulty because of the sheer magnitude of the task. Getting a hundred, a thousand, or ten thousand people to understand and accept a particular vision is usually an enormously challenging undertaking.

For people who have been trained only to be managers, communication of vision can be particularly difficult. Managers tend to think in terms of their immediate subordinates and boss, not the broader constituencies that need to buy into a vision. They tend to be most comfortable with routine factual communication, not future-oriented strategizing and dreaming. Of course, they can learn. But that requires time, effort, and, perhaps most of all, a clear sense of what the problem is and how it can be solved.

THE MAGNITUDE OF THE TASK

Failures to communicate vision are often attributed to either limited intellectual capabilities among lower-level employees or a general human resistance to change, and, hence, to acceptance of information about change. While both of these factors can be relevant, neither gets at the most basic problem.

The development of a transformational vision often requires those on the guiding coalition to spend a few hundred hours collecting information, digesting it, considering alternatives, and eventually making choices. I've seen more than a few cases in which after months of work some of the senior executives involved had great difficulty articulating the latest version of their vision. Not intelligent enough? Hardly. Resisting change? To some degree, yes. But more fundamentally, I think this problem reflects difficulties inherent to the process.

Accepting a vision of the future can be a challenging intellectual and emotional task. Our minds naturally generate dozens of questions. What will this mean for me? My friends? The organization? What other alternatives are there? Are any of the other options better? If I'm going to have to operate differently, can I do it? Will sacrifices from me be required in the process of achieving the vision? How do I feel about those sacrifices? Do I really believe what I'm hearing about a direction for the future? Or are others playing some game, perhaps to improve their positions at my expense?

One of the main reasons that vision creation is such a challenging exercise is that those on the guiding coalition have to answer all these questions for themselves, and that takes time and a lot of communication. The purely intellectual task, the part that could be done by a strategy consultant, is difficult enough, but that often is a minor part of the overall exercise. The emotional work is even tougher: letting go of the status quo, letting go of other future options, coming to grips with the sacrifices, coming to trust others, etc. Yet after they are done with this most difficult work, those on a guiding coalition often act as if everyone else in the organization should become clear and comfortable with the resulting vision in a fraction of that time. So a gallon of information is dumped into a river of routine communication, where it is quickly diluted, lost, and forgotten (see, for example, exhibit 1 on the facing page).

So why do smart people behave this way? Partly, the culprit is old-fashioned condescension. "I'm management. You're labor. I don't expect you to understand anyway." But more important, we undercommunicate because we can't figure out a practical alternative: Put all 10,000 employees through the same exercise as the guiding coalition? Not likely.

The magnitude of the task unnerves people. If the guiding coalition spends a total of 150 hours working on the vision, and if we allow only 20 percent of that for communication to others, that's still 30 hours per person times (let's say) 10,000 people. At $14 an hour for wages and another $6 for benefits, that's $20 x 30 x 10,000 = $6 million. Few firms have room for an additional expense of $6 million in their budgets.

So how do you deal with this problem? Seven principles appear to be closely associated with this stage in a successful transformation (as summarized in exhibit 2 on page 90).

EXHIBIT 1
A Failure to Communicate: How a Change Vision Gets Lost in the Clutter

1. The total amount of communication going to an employee in three months = 2,300,000 words or numbers.

2. The typical communication of a change vision over a period of three months = 13,400 words or numbers (that is, the equivalent of one 30-minute speech, one hour-long meeting, one 600-word article in the firm's newspaper, and one 2,000-word memo).

3. 13,400/2,300,000 = .0058. The change vision captures only .58 percent of the communication market share.

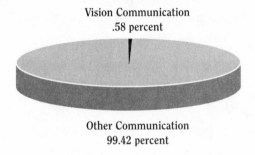

Vision Communication
.58 percent

Other Communication
99.42 percent

KEEP IT SIMPLE

The time and energy required for effective vision communication are directly related to the clarity and simplicity of the message. Focused, jargon-free information can be disseminated to large groups of people at a fraction of the cost of clumsy, complicated communication. Technobabble and MBA-speak just get in the way, creating confusion, suspicion, and alienation. Communication seems to work best when it is so direct and so simple that it has a sort of elegance.

The challenge of simple and direct communication is that it

EXHIBIT 2
Key Elements in the Effective Communication of Vision

➤ *Simplicity:* All jargon and technobabble must be eliminated.

➤ *Metaphor, analogy, and example:* A verbal picture is worth a thousand words.

➤ *Multiple forums:* Big meetings and small, memos and newspapers, formal and informal interaction—all are effective for spreading the word.

➤ *Repetition:* Ideas sink in deeply only after they have been heard many times.

➤ *Leadership by example:* Behavior from important people that is inconsistent with the vision overwhelms other forms of communication.

➤ *Explanation of seeming inconsistencies:* Unaddressed inconsistencies undermine the credibility of all communication.

➤ *Give-and-take:* Two-way communication is always more powerful than one-way communication.

---

requires great clarity of thought plus more than a little courage. Remember the old saw: If I had more time, I'd write you a shorter letter. It's much harder to be clear and concise than overcomplicated and wordy. Simple also means no bamboozling. Technobabble is a shield. If the ideas are dumb, others will recognize them as dumb. Dropping the armor makes us more vulnerable in the short term, which is why we are often reluctant to do so.

A few examples:

Version #1: Our goal is to reduce our mean time to repair parameters so that they are perceptually lower than all major competitors inside the United States and out. In a similar vein, we have targeted new-product development cycle times, order process times, and other customer-relevant processes for change.

Version #2: We are going to become faster than anyone in our industry at satisfying customer needs.

All professions develop a specialized vocabulary, partly out of necessity when needed language doesn't exist, partly as a means of differentiating themselves. Using specialized language helps when you are talking to a brother or sister professional. Similar speech is confusing when you are talking to someone outside the profession. Because most organizations have employees and external constituencies (such as customers and suppliers) that belong to dozens of professions (mechanical engineers, accountants, market researchers, managers), whenever jargon is used, some people will understand and feel included while most of the audience will feel confused and left out. Consequently, all widespread communication in a change effort must be jargon free. When accountants talk only to other accountants, that's a different matter.

Consider two more examples:

Version #1: Through a process of debureaucratization, we will empower our frontline employees to better serve idiosyncratic customer requirements.

Version #2: We are going to throw out some of the rule books and give employees more discretion to do the right thing for our customers.

Use Metaphors, Analogies, Examples

I've often heard people say: Because our company is big and complex, we cannot communicate a sensible vision in a short time using simple language. What these individuals don't understand is the power of metaphor, analogy, example, or just plain colorful language to communicate complicated ideas quickly and effectively.

For example:

Version #1: We need to retain the advantages of economies of great scale and yet become much less bureaucratic and slow in decision making in order to help ourselves retain and win customers in a very competitive and tough business environment (thirty-nine words).

Version #2: We need to become less like an elephant and more like a customer-friendly *Tyrannosaurus rex* (sixteen words).

The image of a vicious dinosaur may seem odd, but for the electronics company that chose it, that idea accurately communicated a great deal. The industry had experienced an explosion of new competition. Small firms were failing each month, and many of the big firms were losing money. The T-rex company decided that it needed to become much more aggressive if it was to survive. The idea of a tiger came to mind, but the company was too big for that to be credible. Besides, size had its advantages if the firm could become fast and tough in the service of customers. Hence, the idea of a customer-friendly *Tyrannosaurus rex.*

If most of the management and employee base in this company liked the image of an elephant or were disgusted by the notion of becoming a T-rex, this communication would have failed. But just the opposite was true. At some hard-to-explain emotional level, most people loved the king-of-dinosaurs idea. It helped them to come to grips with their concerns about change.

Another example:

Version #1: We want to begin designing and manufacturing more products that are perceived by the customer base as different, highly recognizable, and prestigious. Such products will have significantly higher prices and margins (thirty-one words).

Version #2: We are going to be making fewer Fiats and more Mercedes (eleven words).

Again, if the employees valued Fiats more than Mercedes, this communication would fail. Or if they were in some isolated mountain village in Asia and had little experience with these cars, the message would mean little. But neither was the case for the actual company. This simple, eleven-word sentence delivered a great deal of information in an emotionally appealing way.

Well-chosen words can make a message memorable, even if it has to compete with hundreds of other communications for people's attention. Really good advertising people are skilled at this sort of word/image selection. Those of us with degrees in engineering, economics, physical science, or finance are often not. Nevertheless, anyone can draw on the expertise of others. And most people, at least in my experience, can with practice become better at finding imaginative ways to get across their ideas.

USE MANY DIFFERENT FORUMS

Vision is usually communicated most effectively when many different vehicles are used: large group meetings, memos, newspapers, posters, informal one-on-one talks. When the same message comes at people from six different directions, it stands a better chance of being heard and remembered, on both intellectual and emotional levels. So channel A helps answer some of the questions people have, channel B addresses others, and so on.

The cost conscious among us will correctly point out that communication is not free. Although firms occasionally spend a great deal of money on vision communication, most of the successful transformation efforts I've seen exploit the fact that much useless information typically clogs expensive channels of communication. One-third or more of the agenda at the annual management meeting is often dictated by tradition but no longer relevant, or is there to prop up someone's ego, or is in some other way a waste of time. Much of the company newspaper is filler, or ego booster, or propaganda so shameless that it would make the former editors of *Pravda* blush. At least 10 percent of one-on-one conversations every day are about the NBA, a new movie, or golf. Clearing away even some of this talk creates room for important information at no additional cost.

REPEAT, REPEAT, REPEAT

The most carefully crafted messages rarely sink deeply into the recipient's consciousness after only one pronouncement. Our minds are too cluttered, and any communication has to fight hundreds of other ideas for attention. In addition, a single airing won't address all the questions we have. As a result, effective information transferral almost always relies on repetition.

Contrast these two scenarios: In case A, the new vision is introduced as part of three speeches at the annual management meeting and is the subject of three articles in the company newspaper, for a grand total of six repeats over a six-month period. In case B, each of the firm's twenty-five executives pledges to find four opportunities per day to tie conversations back to the big picture. So when Hiro is meeting with his top twenty people to review monthly results versus plan, he asks that all decisions be evaluated in light of the new vision, which he repeats. When Gloria does performance evaluations for her employees, she ties her assessments to major change initiatives. When Jan conducts a Q and A at a plant, he answers the first inquiry by saying: "I think yes, but let me explain why. The vision directing our change efforts is . . ." The net result: twenty-five executives, four times a day, over six months equals more than 12,000 repeats. Six versus 12,000.

All successful cases of major change seem to include tens of thousands of communications that help employees to grapple with difficult intellectual and emotional issues. This happens not because the public relations department takes on "vision distribution" as a "project." This happens because dozens of managers, supervisors, and executives look at all of their daily activities through the lens of the new vision. When people do this, they can easily find many meaningful ways to talk about the direction of change, communications that can always be tailored to the specific person or group with whom they are talking.

Willie and three of his people are walking to a meeting when they pass a new poster on the wall about the quality program. Willie points and asks them, "What do you think? Does this get the point across? What does this say to you?" Frances and fifteen of her people are in a conference room listening to a request for funds. When the formal presentation is over, she asks: "How does this relate to all the reengineering work? As I understand it, the vision guiding those efforts is . . ." Todd is in a cafeteria addressing 200 employees. He is asked: "Do you think the number of people we employ here might ever go up?" His response: "If we are successful in implementing our vision, the answer will surely be yes. Is that vision clear to you? Is it credible?"

A sentence here, a paragraph there, two minutes in the middle of a meeting, five minutes at the end of a conversation, three quick references in a speech—collectively, these brief mentions can add up to a massive amount of useful communication, which is generally what is needed to win over both hearts and minds.

WALK THE TALK, OR LEAD BY EXAMPLE

Often the most powerful way to communicate a new direction is through behavior. When the top five or fifty people all live the change vision, employees will usually grasp it better than if there had been a hundred stories in the in-house newsletter. When they see top management acting out the vision, a whole set of troublesome questions about credibility and game playing tends to evaporate.

Consider this example: The central element in a new transformation effort at a major airline relates to customer service. Whenever the CEO receives a letter of complaint from a customer, he personally sends a response back within forty-eight hours. After a while, stories about his letters circulate throughout the company. The net result: An outside research firm finds that 90 percent of the employees can describe the change vision when asked and nearly 80 percent say that they believe senior management is committed to making it a reality.

Another example: The change effort at a huge European manufacturing company focuses on creating a flatter, leaner firm. At about the same time that the new direction is first communicated to employees, senior management eliminates one level at the top of the hierarchy—executive vice presidents—and announces that headquarters staff will be reduced by 50 percent over a period of eighteen months through attrition, early retirements, and job cutting. Soon afterward, a consulting firm finds that a high percentage of lower-level employees can correctly describe the direction of change in the company.

Another example: A general is trying to communicate to a gigantic organization that defense budgets are shrinking and that everyone must become more frugal. So when he travels, instead of climbing into a U.S. Army Blackhawk helicopter outside the Pentagon and then onto a dedicated USAF C-12 jet at Andrews Air Force Base, he does the following as often as possible: He descends to the basement of the Pentagon, boards the subway for 80 cents to Washington National Airport, takes a shuttle to the terminal, and then rides coach on a commercial airline. The word of his travels spreads fast.

We often call such behavior "leadership by example." The concept is simple. Words are cheap, but action is not. The cynical among us, in particular, tend not to believe words but will be impressed by action.

In a similar vein, telling people one thing and then behaving differently is a great way to undermine the communication of a change vision. Division head Sally O'Rourke tells her 1,200 employees that speed, speed, speed should become the hallmark of their organization. Then she takes nine months to approve a capital request from one of her product managers, allowing the competition to grab the lion's share of the market in a new and expanding segment. CEO John Jones preaches lower costs, lower costs, lower costs. Then he has his office remodeled for

$150,000. Executive vice president Harold Rose talks endlessly about customer service, but when complaints about a new product flood in and an inquiring reporter from the *Wall Street Journal* calls, he defends his product instead of his customers.

In short: *Nothing undermines the communication of a change vision more than behavior on the part of key players that seems inconsistent with the vision.* The implications are powerful: (1) Trying to sell a vision before top management can embody it is tough; and (2) even under the best of circumstances, carefully monitoring senior management behavior is a good idea so that you can identify and address inconsistencies between words and deeds.

EXPLICITLY ADDRESS SEEMING INCONSISTENCIES

I recently visited a bank that was undergoing major cost-cutting initiatives as a part of a broader transformation effort. Employees were feeling the pain and were understandably sensitive to any sign that management wasn't doing its share. Unfortunately, those signs were everywhere.

While productivity task forces seemed to be slashing costs twenty-four hours a day, the corporation continued to lease six jets for executive use. While a hundred employees were laid off here, another hundred there, top management presided in regal quarters. While Christmas parties were being cancelled at some locations to save money, the CEO flew his entire board first class to London for one of its meetings.

When I point out such inconsistencies, executives either roll their eyes or become extremely defensive. "What are you saying? You want us to pry the wood off the walls and make this place (headquarters) look shabby?" "We've done the analysis six times, and the jets keep looking like a good deal. Without them, there's no way to get to some remote plants. You really think it's a good use of a busy person's time to go to an airport, wait for a commercial jet, transfer at the other end to a commuter jet, and then drive two hours?" "A part of our vision is to internationalize the business, so we have got to globalize the board. That's why we're meeting in London. Do you want a board that thinks only in terms of the U.S.?"

Executives become frustrated when asked to defend the jets, the mahogany, and the overseas trips because they can see no easy way to deal with these issues. They don't want to encourage cynicism among employees, but selling headquarters, cancelling the leases, and forgetting London doesn't make sense to them. "We really did look into selling the building, but the disruption and relocation costs are significant. So what do we do?" In some cases, the answer is ditch the offices, jets, and trips. But in other instances, that won't be practical or sensible. Then the answer is to explicitly address the issues in honest communication. For example:

> With all the cost cutting that is going on out of necessity throughout the company, it is inexcusable for any of us to be wasting money, especially on unneeded luxuries. Within this context, we have decided that the offices and furnishings for our executives are not justifiable. At present, selling headquarters and moving to less luxurious surroundings would cost more than it would save. But we will continue to look for a cost-effective and practical way to reduce this sign of excess.

Straightforward and honest messages are often laughed at by cynics. If most employees are highly suspicious of management, then such messages won't help. But for the employee who wants to believe in his or her company, such a communication is usually much appreciated. Credibility and trust increase, which in turn contribute to communicating the change vision.

Q: Why don't people do this sort of thing more often?
A: They are doing it more and more often.

Imperial, feed-the-mushrooms-manure styles of management are dying out. In a fast-moving world, where there's a need to engage employees' hearts and minds, uncommunicative executives will not be able to transform their firms into tough competitors. Because we've all seen situations in which withholding information or just plain telling lies seemed to help someone win, we are all somewhat skeptical of this observation. But it's the truth.

In successful transformations, important inconsistencies in the messages employees are getting are almost always addressed explicitly. If mixed signals can't be eliminated, they are usually explained, simply and honestly.

LISTEN AND BE LISTENED TO

Because the communication of vision is often such a difficult activity, it can easily turn into a screeching, one-way broadcast in which useful feedback is ignored and employees are inadvertently made to feel unimportant. In highly successful change efforts, this rarely happens, because communication always becomes a two-way endeavor.

I've seen more than a few cases in which guiding coalitions didn't get the vision exactly right and some employees figured this out or could have solved the problems had they been well informed. Yet because feedback wasn't solicited, the errors were never corrected until late in the process. In one instance in particular, this problem proved to be enormously costly in terms of unnecessary information technology expenses. A half-dozen computerwise young sales reps would have seen immediately, had they been briefed, that the basic concept guiding new hardware and software purchases for the sales force was flawed. But they were never briefed until after the new equipment arrived. By then, after a less computer-literate middle management had accepted and implemented a faulty vision, course corrections were very costly.

Even more fundamentally, two-way discussions are an essential method of helping people answer all the questions that occur to them in a transformation effort. Clear, simple, memorable, often repeated, consistent communication from multiple sources, modeled by executive behavior, helps enormously. But most human beings, especially well-educated ones, buy into something only after they have had a chance to wrestle with it. Wrestling means asking questions, challenging, and arguing. This, of course, is precisely what happens when the vision is first created by the guiding coalition.

Change initiators sometimes avoid two-way communication because of concerns over cost. Their logic is straightforward; whatever the expense for one-way information flow, double that—at a minimum—for two-way. They correctly point out that everyone can't be put through the same experience as the guiding coalition. But here again they overlook the usefulness of getting as many managers as possible to view hourly events through the lens of the new vision. When people do so, they invariably find dozens of inexpensive ways to generate dialogue around the vision. Five minutes in a product launch meeting, two minutes in a hallway conversation, ten minutes at the end of a speech—the minutes can add up to thousands of hours.

As change initiators, we sometimes also avoid this activity because we are afraid our visions won't survive two rounds in a ring. Such behavior is understandable, but regrettable.

If people don't accept a vision, the next two steps in the transformation process—empowering individuals for broad-based action and creating short-term wins—will fail. Employees will neither take advantage of their empowerment nor put in the effort to guarantee the wins. Worse yet, if they accept and then attempt to implement a poorly formulated vision, as in the information technology example, precious time and resources will be wasted and many people will suffer the consequences.

The downside of two-way communication is that feedback may suggest that we are on the wrong course and that the vision needs to be reformulated. But in the long run, swallowing our pride and reworking the vision is far more productive than heading off in the wrong direction—or in a direction that others won't follow.

CHAPTER 7

Empowering Employees for Broad-Based Action

➤ **"I**F I HEAR THE WORD *EMPOWER-ment* one more time," someone recently told me, "I think I'll gag." He was expressing exasperation at the fact that the more this increasingly popular term is used, the less it seems to mean. "It's become a politically correct mantra," he said. "Empower, empower, empower. I ask people what they mean by that and they either become inarticulate or they look at me like I'm an idiot."

A few years ago, I might have agreed with his reservations. Today, I don't. I'm still not enthusiastic about using faddish words, but in this ever faster-moving world, I think the idea of helping more people to become more powerful is important.

Environmental change demands organizational change.

EXHIBIT 1

Barriers to Empowerment

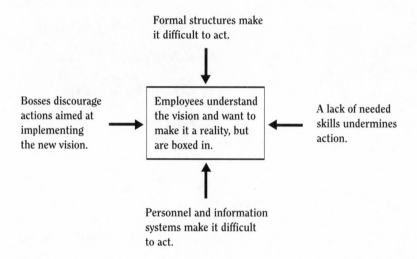

Formal structures make it difficult to act.

Bosses discourage actions aimed at implementing the new vision.

Employees understand the vision and want to make it a reality, but are boxed in.

A lack of needed skills undermines action.

Personnel and information systems make it difficult to act.

Major internal transformation rarely happens unless many people assist. Yet employees generally won't help, or can't help, if they feel relatively powerless. Hence the relevance of empowerment.

Effectively completing stages 1 through 4 of the transformation process already does a great deal to empower people. But even when urgency is high, a guiding coalition has created an appropriate vision, and the vision has been well communicated, numerous obstacles can still stop employees from creating needed change. The purpose of stage 5 is to empower a broad base of people to take action by removing as many barriers to the implementation of the change vision as possible at this point in the process.

What are the biggest obstacles that often need to be attacked? Four can be particularly important: structures, skills, systems, and supervisors (see exhibit 1 above).

REMOVING STRUCTURAL BARRIERS

The firm in this case is a financial services organization in Australia. A new president pushes up the urgency rate, assembles a guiding coalition at the top, and helps it develop a new direction for the company that is centered around superior customer service. The basic concept is simple: to develop a capability that will not just gain share in Australia but that will allow the firm to compete effectively in emerging markets throughout Asia. The team's success in communicating the new vision leaves many employees convinced that the firm is on the right path. When top management sees the enthusiastic response to its initiatives, its members conclude that the most difficult part of the transformation process may be over—which is probably why they take their collective eye off the ball.

Twenty-four months later, a frustrated and angry group of senior managers tries to assess what went wrong. They felt they had been doing their part. They had been visiting customers throughout the region, helping set up new systems to measure customer satisfaction, making speeches inside the firm to reinforce the customer service message, and working with consultants to redesign products and services to better meet marketplace requirements. But for some reason, the once enthusiastic troops just aren't delivering.

A postmortem finds the following. Many employees really did want to provide superior products and services, and they tried. But the organizational structure so fragmented resources and authority that delivering well any of the new financial products was nearly impossible. A typical product required people from four different functional organizations to work together seamlessly. Even when employees tried to create cross-functional teams that were product/customer focused, they found the process enormously frustrating. Strong structural silos undermined the teams in dozens of subtle ways, making the timely delivery of new services to customers virtually impossible. When employees complained to their supervisors, they were told that they should try to be better team players. When they suggested that perhaps the organizational structure was a problem, they were given a dozen excuses about why changing the structure was not possible, or wouldn't help, or would take a long time. Disempowered, they gave up trying to implement the new vision.

When the CEO in this case confronted his managers with the structural problem and asked for their advice, they told him:

1. implementation of the new vision was a complicated affair,

2. they might have the wrong kind of employee, which would take a very long time to correct,

3. middle management was exhausted after putting in long hours trying to do the right thing, and

4. there was no obvious solution to these problems.

To some degree, all of this was true. Long workweeks were common, for example, but key people in middle management were also stressed out from trying to preserve their functional fiefdoms despite mounting evidence that a reorganization would be necessary to deliver the new products and services. As is so often the case with change, resistance didn't come from everyone. Only a few managers were really dragging their feet. But they were difficult to influence, partly because they had convinced themselves that they were doing the right thing for the company.

Colin was typical of the footdraggers. After twenty-five years of experience, he well understood the virtues of the functional organization in which he had invested so much time and energy. The various schemes for reorganization not only broke up his group and greatly reduced the size of his job, they also eliminated some of the business benefits of the traditional structure. Had Colin completely embraced the new vision, he would have reluctantly had to agree that losses from a restructuring were not that significant. But he saw the vision as a pleasant dream

---

EXHIBIT 2
How Structure Can Undermine Vision

THE VISION	THE STRUCTURE
➤ Focus on the customer	➤ But the organization fragments resources and responsibility for products and services
➤ Give more responsibility to lower-level employees	➤ But there are layers of middle-level managers who second-guess and criticize employees
➤ Increase productivity to become the low-cost producer	➤ But huge staff groups at corporate headquarters are expensive and constantly initiate costly procedures and programs
➤ Speed everything up	➤ But independent silos don't communicate and thus slow everything down

with about a one-in-four chance of being realized. So with the losses clear and certain and the potential gains foggy and improbable, he dragged his feet. The net result was that the company retained an organization structure that systematically blocked employee efforts to implement the new vision.

Structure is not always a big barrier in transformations, at least in the early stages, but I've seen many cases in which organizational arrangements undermine a vision by disempowering people (as listed in exhibit 2 above). The case of the Australian financial services firm is not uncommon. Customer-focused visions often fail unless customer-*un*focused organizational structures are modified. Another typical example would be an electrical utility whose vision of frontline employees taking on much more responsibility bumps up against a structure with too many levels and too much decision-making authority vested in the middle. As employees try to make the new vision a reality, their decisions are second-guessed and undermined by a hoard of middle managers. "Did you take this into consideration?" "You should have checked with Jones first." "Do you realize the precedent you might be setting?" Predictably, after a while, most frontline employees give up and revert back to their old ways of operating.

Whenever structural barriers are not removed in a timely way, the risk is that employees will become so frustrated that they will sour on the entire transformational effort. If that happens, even if you eventually reorganize correctly, you've lost the energy needed to use the new structure to make the vision a reality.

Why does this happen? Sometimes we become so accustomed to one basic organizational design, perhaps because it has been used for decades, that we are blind to the alternatives. Sometimes people have so much invested in one structure, in terms of personal loyalties and functional expertise, that they are afraid of the potential career consequences. Sometimes senior managers know a redesign is needed, but they don't want to get into a fight with middle management or with their peers. But often the basis for change hasn't been firmly enough established. Middle management easily resists structural change when it doesn't feel a sense of urgency, doesn't see a dedicated team at the top, doesn't see a sensible vision for change, or doesn't feel that others believe in that vision.

PROVIDING NEEDED TRAINING

Nearly twenty years ago I watched a forward-thinking automotive parts company try to make major changes in its manufacturing operations in order to leapfrog the competition. Long before others were taking layers out of middle management and giving more authority to lower-level employees, this firm had a vision of how such an approach could improve quality and lower costs. The guiding coalition made many mistakes, as pioneers always do, but successfully built a plant in the rural Southeast that was thin on middle management, largely run by teams of workers, and clearly ahead of its time. Getting the factory up and running was not easy, but no one was surprised by that. After reaching about 70 percent of the daily output target, plant management assumed the hard work was over. It wasn't.

Output leveled off at 75 percent of target, an economically unacceptable result. The workforce became increasingly grumpy. Fights actually broke out in one of the manufacturing teams. Managers who had been skeptical about the experiment began to wonder out loud if "workers" could really handle "managerial" responsibility. A few disgruntled employees began listening to union overtures. Someone at corporate headquarters suggested that they "pull the plug" on this new method of operation before events spun out of control.

As is so often the case, a few people in the factory had correctly diagnosed the problem, but others weren't listening to them. The plant manager eventually talked to nearly everyone and then decided that a junior employee-relations specialist had the best explanation for why they were stuck at 75 percent. In essence, that young man said:

> We have taken 200 people, managers and workers, and put them into a situation that is different from anything they had experienced before. All of them, especially the older ones, have some habits built up over years that are no longer relevant, sometimes even dysfunctional. Many of our workers have learned relatively sophisticated skills associated with ducking responsibility. None of them know much about operating effectively in teams in a work setting. Most of our managers have been taught by five to thirty-five years of experience that their job is to make decisions, not empower others. The amount of training we received to cope with this new situation seems, in retrospect, woefully inadequate. Because most of us wanted very much to make the new

plant successful, we worked exceptionally hard during start-up. In a way, we used sheer effort to make up for lack of skills. But that's not a long-term solution. We got tired, and then frustrated.

Today this problem is often seen in major reengineering efforts. Training is provided, but it's not enough, or it's not the right kind, or it's not done at the right time. People are expected to change habits built up over years or decades with only five days of education. People are taught technical skills but not the social skills or attitudes needed to make the new arrangements work. People are given a course before they start their new jobs, but aren't provided with follow-up to help them with problems they encounter while performing those jobs.

I think there are two common reasons why we fall into this trap. First, we often don't think through carefully enough what new behavior, skills, and attitudes will be needed when major changes are initiated. As a result, we don't recognize the kind and amount of training that will be required to help people learn those new behaviors, skills, and attitudes. Second, we sometimes do recognize correctly what is needed, but when we translate that into time and money, we are overwhelmed by the results. How can anyone justify sending 10,000 people to a two-day training course? Or spend $3 million on a special educational effort?

Two of the most successful transformations in the world in the mid-1980s involved European airlines that did send tens of thousands of people to two-day training sessions and that did spend millions of dollars in the process. In both cases, the companies were pursuing new customer-first visions. In both cases, the guiding coalitions concluded that important attitudinal changes were needed to implement the visions and strategies. The two-day course, exceptionally well designed by a Danish consulting firm, was not meant to be a one-shot panacea for all the behavioral, skill-related, and attitudinal problems. Instead, a series of lectures and exercises simply demonstrated how behavior that "put people first" paid off greatly in life, both on and off the job. All the evidence I've seen strongly suggests that this training was a critical element in empowering employees to put the new visions to work. And both airlines emerged from the process as much stronger and more successful competitors.

As in the case of the airlines, attitude training is often just as important as skills training. Over the past century, millions of nonmanagerial employees have been taught by their companies and their unions not to accept much responsibility. For many of these people, you can't just say, "OK, now you're empowered, go to it." Some simply won't believe you, some will think it's an exploitative trick, and others will worry that they aren't capable. New experiences are needed to erase corrosive beliefs, and some of that can be done efficiently with training.

I see no evidence that all organizations should spend millions on education during attempts at major change. In some cases, big training budgets are unnecessary because large numbers of people are not being asked to learn significantly new skills, behaviors, or attitudes. In many cases, clever design of educational experiences can deliver greater impact at one-half or less the cost of conventional approaches. I also think that training can easily become a disempowering experience if the implicit message is "shut up and do it this way" instead of "we will be delegating more, so we are providing this course to help you with your new responsibilities."

The point is: Some training could be required at this stage in a transformation, but it needs to be the right kind of experience. Throwing money at the problem is never a good idea, nor is talking down to people.

ALIGNING SYSTEMS TO THE VISION

"We've done everything," one manager tells me, "but they just keep resisting."

"OK," I say, "tell me more."

"We've worked enormously hard to develop an exciting concept for what we want to become. We've communicated those ideas endlessly through every mechanism we could think of. We reorganized last year to make the structure consistent with the new concept. Where necessary, we've retrained people. All this has demanded great time and energy, but we've done it."

"So what's the problem?"

"Far too many people are still conducting business the old way," he complains.

"Why do you think that is?"

"I'm beginning to suspect that it's just human nature to resist change."

"If you won the lottery for $10 million," I ask, "would you refuse to accept the money?"

"Are you kidding?"

"But there is plenty of evidence that when people win a lot of money their lives change in some pretty important ways."

"So?"

"So you're telling me you wouldn't resist that change."

"OK, OK," he says. "So maybe people don't resist all kinds of change."

"When don't they resist?"

"I suppose if they see it's in their best interests."

"And do your HR systems make it in people's best interests to implement your new vision?"

"HR systems?"

"Performance appraisal. Compensation. Promotions. Succession planning. Are they aligned with the new vision?"

"Well, maybe not entirely."

Examination of this firm's human resource systems reveals:

➤ The performance evaluation form has virtually nothing about customers on it, yet that is at the core of the new vision.
➤ Compensation decisions are based much more on not making mistakes than on creating useful change.
➤ Promotion decisions are made in a highly subjective way and seem to have at best a limited relationship to the change effort.

➤ Recruiting and hiring systems are a decade old and only marginally support the transformation.

Further investigation also shows that management information systems haven't changed much to help the transformation; likewise the strategic planning process, which still focuses much too much on short-term financial information and much too little on market/competitive analysis.

During the first half of a major change effort, owing to constraints on time, energy, and/or money, you can't alter everything. Barriers associated with the organization's culture, for example, are extremely difficult to remove completely until the end of each change project, after performance improvements are clear. Systems are easier to move, but if you tried to iron out every little inconsistency between the new vision and the current systems, you'd simply fail. Before some solid short-term wins are established, the guiding coalition rarely has the momentum or power to make that much change. Nevertheless, when the big, built-in, hard-wired incentives and processes are seriously at odds with the new vision, you must deal with that fact directly. Dodging the issue disempowers employees and risks undermining the change.

Q: How often do the systems, especially the HR systems, get in the way?
A: Far too often.

History often leaves HR people in highly bureaucratic personnel functions that discourage leadership and make altering human resource practices a big challenge. Breaking out of this pattern is not easy. Yet in successful transformations, I increasingly see gutsy HR men and women helping provide the leadership needed to change the systems to fit a new vision. In some cases they do so despite little encouragement from line managers or even from their HR colleagues. They do so because they care deeply about employees and are appalled by the consequences of poorly handled change efforts.

DEALING WITH TROUBLESOME SUPERVISORS

Frank doesn't seem to get it. He's been told a dozen times that the company is trying to become more innovative because creativity is paying off greatly in its industry. But he refuses to change a command-and-control style that snuffs out initiative and creativity as quickly as carbon dioxide kills a fire. Watching him operate, you might wonder if he didn't get a degree in disempowerment. "We've tried that before," he says again and again. "You need to do more analysis on the downside possibilities," he tells his people. "We don't have time for that, just do this please." "Yeah, yeah, that's very interesting, but . . . No, no, don't send that report around; people don't need that information." "Please Martha, next time check with me first before you do anything."

Frank runs a department with about a hundred employees. Waves of change wash up to his door, break, and then retreat out to sea. A few of his people try to support the corporate renewal program despite Frank's best efforts. But most don't. Some tried initially and then gave up. Some, like Frank, just don't get it. Others are cautious and political and take their cue from the boss.

Change zealots tend to demonize Frank, but he's not really a bad person. To a large degree, like all of us, he's a product of his history. He learned a command-and-control style early on, and because that behavior seemed to work and help him get ahead in the company, it developed into a deeply ingrained set of habits.

If Frank's problem were related to only a single discrete element, change would come much more easily. But that's not the case. He has dozens of interrelated habits that add up to a style of management. If he alters just one aspect of his behavior, all the other interrelated elements tend to put great pressure on him to switch that one piece of behavior back to the way it was. What he needs is to change all the habits as a group, but that can feel as hard as trying to quit smoking, drinking, and eating fatty foods all at the same time.

The fact that Frank doesn't entirely believe in the new "innovation" vision makes all this even more difficult, as does the fact that he's not entirely sure what he would need to do to help implement that vision. And, like all of us, he's skilled at rationalizing the situation so that, in his own eyes, he looks like the good corporate citizen while others are political, self-serving, or incompetent.

People like Frank seem to exist in all cases of reengineering, restructuring, or strategic change. If there are enough of them, or if they are in charge of enough employees, they can be a huge problem. If particularly powerful people like Frank are not confronted early in a change process, they can undermine the entire effort.

I've seen at least a dozen cases where three or four key players were Frank-like. Instead of confronting the problem, an enthusiastic change agent and a few colleagues dragged those people through stages 1 to 4 of a transformation. But in stage 5, the refusal of these supervisors to let go and empower their employees finally brought a strained effort to a halt.

One major reason why the Franks of the world aren't confronted is that others are afraid that these people can't change, yet they are unwilling to demote or fire them. Sometimes the unwillingness to act is driven by guilt, especially if the disempowerers are friends or former mentors. Political considerations also play a big role in these cases. People fear that if a fight erupts, the Franks may be powerful enough to win, perhaps even forcing the change agents out. In many other situations, the reluctance to act is related to the good short-term results delivered by people like Frank.

Easy solutions to this sort of problem often don't exist. Faced with that reality, managers sometimes concoct incredibly complicated political strategies. They try to manipulate the Franks into a corner where they can be contained or killed off. The problem with such an approach is that it is often slow, and if exposed to daylight it can look terrible—sleazy, cruel, unfair.

From what I've seen, the best solution to this kind of problem is usually honest dialogue. Here's the story with the industry, the company, our vision, the assistance we need from you, and the time frame in which we need all this. What can we do to help you help us? If the situation really is hopeless, and the person needs to be replaced, that fact often becomes clear early in this dialogue. If the person wants to help but feels blocked, the discussion can identify solutions. If the person wants to help but is incapable of doing so, the clearer expectations and timetable can eventually make his or her removal less contentious. The basic fairness of this approach helps overcome guilt. The rational and thoughtful dialogue also helps minimize the risk that good short-term results will suddenly turn bad or that Frank and others like him will be able to launch a successful political counterattack.

Guilt, political considerations, and concerns over short-term results stop people all the time from having these honest discussions. In retrospect, executives often express regret that they didn't confront problem managers sooner in the process. If I've heard it once, I've heard it a hundred times: "I should have dealt with Hal/George/Irene much earlier."

An unwillingness to confront managers like Frank is common in change efforts. It rarely helps. These blockers stop needed action. Perhaps even more important, others see that these people are not being confronted and they become discouraged. Discouraged employees do not produce the short-term wins that are vital to building momentum in a transformation effort. Discouraged employees do not help manage the large number of change projects that typically are needed in a transformation. Instead, they give up long before you have reached the finish line and anchored new approaches in the organization's culture.

TAPPING AN ENORMOUS SOURCE OF POWER

Discouraged and disempowered employees never make enterprises winners in a globalizing economic environment. But with the right structure, training, systems, and supervisors to build

---

EXHIBIT 3
Empowering People to Effect Change

➤ *Communicate a sensible vision to employees:* If employees have a shared sense of purpose, it will be easier to initiate actions to achieve that purpose.

➤ *Make structures compatible with the vision:* Unaligned structures block needed action.

➤ *Provide the training employees need:* Without the right skills and attitudes, people feel disempowered.

➤ *Align information and personnel systems to the vision:* Unaligned systems also block needed action.

➤ *Confront supervisors who undercut needed change:* Nothing disempowers people the way a bad boss can.

on a well-communicated vision (see exhibit 3 above), increasing numbers of firms are finding that they can tap an enormous source of power to improve organizational performance. They can mobilize hundreds or thousands of people to help provide leadership to produce needed changes.

CHAPTER 8

Generating Short-Term Wins

➤ **W**HEN ONE OF THE MOST
visionary, charismatic executives
I've known was appointed president of a $1.7 billion division of a
large U.S. company, the level of
excitement at that business rose
dramatically. To many employees,
his first year felt like a wonderful
and needed breath of fresh air.
Suddenly, bold ideas were discussed in meetings instead of
seeming trivialities. Sacred cows
were herded away, and anyone
with valid information on problems or opportunities was given a
hearing. As a coalition of people
emerged around the new leader,
that team began talking of shifts
in the fundamental strategic
direction of the firm.

A vision of a global powerhouse
began to emerge, a firm that
would exploit new technologies to
offer some basic, high-quality
building materials at remarkably

low prices. By the middle of year two, communication about the new vision permeated every part of the organization. By the beginning of year three, more and more changes were being made to help convert the vision into reality. New products were launched. New training programs were introduced. Departments were reorganized. A major reengineering effort was begun in the finance function. One key executive took an early retirement. Nearly $500 million was spent on a major acquisition. All the activity was exhilarating. Even the business press loved it; in the middle of year three, four different publications ran flattering articles about the changes being made at that firm.

This story impressed me greatly. Not that I didn't see some red flags. Our hero's guiding coalition was never linked very strongly to corporate headquarters. But so much of what he was doing was right on target that if you had asked me during year three, I would probably have said that this business would become the leader in its industry within the next forty-eight months. I couldn't imagine that the transformation process could be derailed.

I was wrong.

To make a long story short, in the middle of year four, the charismatic leader was fired. Over the next twelve months, many of his initiatives collapsed and disappeared. During that time, probably two or three other managers were forced out of the firm, and at least a half-dozen more left on their own accord. Employee morale collapsed. Financial results actually improved for a few quarters before beginning a long march downward. As I write this, the division is still a mess.

With the benefit of hindsight, the errors are easy to spot. Only one executive at corporate headquarters was a part of the guiding coalition, and he wasn't a particularly influential individual. By the middle of year two, people who disagreed with that coalition were ignored, even if they were trying to be helpful. But the worst mistake was that insufficient attention was given to short-term results. People became so caught up in big dreams that they didn't effectively manage the current reality. When critics asked for evidence that all this activity was moving the firm in the right direction, despite few if any performance improvements, nothing convincing was offered. When the coalition accused the disgruntled of being a bunch of unvisionary poops, corporate headquarters grew wary. When the division missed almost all of its financial projections in year three by a small amount, without warning corporate much in advance, the CEO grew wary. When the division lost money in the second quarter of year four, again without much warning, the charismatic division president was fired.

Some people both inside and outside of this company still think the CEO made a terrible mistake. They could be right. But the charismatic division general manager unquestionably made one major error. By putting almost no emphasis on short-term results, he didn't build the credibility he needed to sustain his efforts over the long haul.

Major change takes time, sometimes lots of time. Zealous believers will often stay the course no matter what happens. Most of the rest of us expect to see convincing evidence that all the effort is paying off. Nonbelievers have even higher standards of proof. They want to see clear data indicating that the changes are working and that the change process isn't absorbing so many resources in the short term as to endanger the organization.

Running a transformation effort without serious attention to short-term wins is extremely risky (see exhibit 1 on the following page). Sometimes you get lucky; visible results just happen. But sometimes your luck runs out, as it did for the visionary division general manager.

THE USEFULNESS OF SHORT-TERM WINS: AN EXAMPLE

An insurance company has a huge reengineering effort under way. Aware that the project will take at least four years to complete, those on the guiding coalition ask themselves, How can we target and then produce some unambiguous performance

EXHIBIT 1

The Influence of Short-Term Wins on Business Transformation

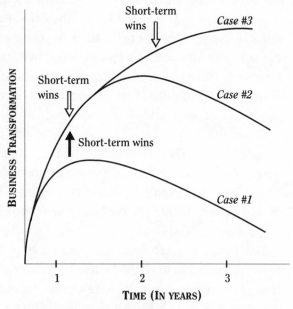

Case #1: No short-term wins

Case #2: Short-term wins at about fourteen months, but none a year later

Case #3: Short-term wins at fourteen and twenty-six months

improvements in six to eighteen months? With careful thought, they identify three areas: one department in which costs could drop significantly within a year, a process improvement that should be quickly visible to and liked by customers, and a small reorganization that should improve morale in one group. For each of the three areas, specific goals and plans are built into the company's two-year operating budget. One person in the coalition is given responsibility for monitoring all three efforts. In executive committee meetings, at least once every sixty days all three miniprojects are reviewed.

Realizing these performance improvements within the short-term time frame turns out to be a challenge. Middle management tries to delay the reorganization. Even the zealots driving the reengineering effort want to slow down the process improvements that would be visible to customers. Complicating all this, the company's information systems do not always track the correct data on which improvements can be shown. Had someone not actively managed these performance issues, the firm in this case would probably never have had three unambiguous short-term wins. Various pressures would have caused delays or changed the agenda. Existing systems would have failed to track the data needed to demonstrate the gains clearly.

Even with these wins, skeptics were able to find some evidence that the reengineering was too costly, too slow, or simply wrongheaded. But the performance improvements knocked air out of their sails. Creating those wins also provided the guiding coalition with concrete feedback about the validity of their vision. And for those who were working so hard to produce meaningful change, planning for the short-term results provided milestones they could look forward to while achieving the actual wins gave them a chance to pat themselves on the back.

THE NATURE AND TIMING OF SHORT-TERM WINS

The kind of results required in stage 6 of a transformation process are both visible and unambiguous. Subtlety won't help. Close calls don't either.

Having a good meeting usually doesn't qualify as the kind of unambiguous win needed in this phase, nor does getting two people to stop fighting, producing a new design that the engineering manager thinks is terrific, or sending 5,000 copies of a new vision statement around the company. Any of these actions may be important, but none is a good example of a short-term win.

A good short-term win has at least these three characteristics:

1. It's visible; large numbers of people can see for themselves whether the result is real or just hype.

2. It's unambiguous; there can be little argument over the call.

3. It's clearly related to the change effort.

When a reengineering effort promises that the first cost reductions will come in twelve months and they occur as predicted, that's a win. When a reorganization early in a transformation reduces the first phase of the new-product development cycle from ten to three months, that's a win. When the early assimilation of an acquisition is handled so well that *Business Week* writes a complimentary story, that's a win.

In small companies or in small units of enterprises, the first results are often needed in half a year. In big organizations, some unambiguous wins are required by eighteen months. Regardless of size, this means that you're probably still not out of most of the early stages when phase 6 has to produce something.

Q: But isn't operating in multiple stages at once complicated?
A: Yes. But that's what happens in successful cases of major change.

THE ROLE OF SHORT-TERM WINS

Short-term performance improvements help transformations in at least six ways (as summarized in exhibit 2 on the facing page). First, they give the effort needed reinforcement. They show people that the sacrifices are paying off, that they are getting stronger.

Second, for those driving the change, these little wins offer an opportunity to relax for a few minutes and celebrate. Constant tension for long periods of time is not healthy for people. The little celebration following a win can be good for the body and spirit.

Third, the process of producing short-term wins can help a guiding coalition test its vision against concrete conditions. What is learned in these tests can be extremely valuable. Sometimes the vision isn't entirely right. More often, the strate-

---

EXHIBIT 2
The Role of Short-Term Wins

➤ *Provide evidence that sacrifices are worth it:* Wins greatly help justify the short-term costs involved.

➤ *Reward change agents with a pat on the back:* After a lot of hard work, positive feedback builds morale and motivation.

➤ *Help fine-tune vision and strategies:* Short-term wins give the guiding coalition concrete data on the viability of their ideas.

➤ *Undermine cynics and self-serving resisters:* Clear improvements in performance make it difficult for people to block needed change.

➤ *Keep bosses on board:* Provides those higher in the hierarchy with evidence that the transformation is on track.

➤ *Build momentum:* Turns neutrals into supporters, reluctant supporters into active helpers, etc.

---

gies need some adjustments. Without the concentrated effort to produce short-term wins, such problems can become apparent far too late in the game.

Fourth, quick performance improvements undermine the efforts of cynics and major league resisters. Wins don't necessarily quiet all of these people (which is probably good, since diversity of opinion can keep a firm from blindly walking off a cliff), but they take some of the ammunition out of opponents' hands and make it much more difficult to take cheap shots at those trying to implement needed changes. As a general rule, the more cynics and resisters, the more important are short-term wins.

Fifth, visible results help retain the essential support of bosses. From middle management all the way up to the board of directors, if those hierarchically above a transformation effort lose faith, it's in deep trouble.

Finally, and perhaps most generally, short-term wins help build necessary momentum. Fence sitters are transformed into supporters, reluctant supporters into active participants, and so on. This momentum is critical, because, as we'll see in the next chapter, the energy needed to complete stage 7 is often enormous.

PLANNING VERSUS PRAYING FOR RESULTS

Transformations sometimes go off track because people simply don't appreciate the role that quick performance improvements play in a change effort. But more often the effort is undermined because managers don't systematically plan for the creation of short-term wins.

"So what kind of evidence do you think we'll see within twenty-four months that all this is on track?" I ask.

"There are four or five possibilities," a member of the guiding coalition replies.

"Possibilities?" I say.

"Yes. With a little luck, costs will be significantly down in either the order processing areas or the order fulfillment group."

"A little luck," I say.

"If marketing can get its act together fast enough, we might see some real revenue increases by then because of the new niching strategies."

"You might?"

"Yes. And it's possible, I suppose, that the new ad agency—we're selecting one now—will have implemented enough of the TV strategy to show some measurable market share improvement."

"It's possible?"

"Yes, any of that might happen."

In highly successful change efforts, you don't hear much dialogue like this. Short-term wins don't come about as the result of a little luck. They aren't merely possibilities. People don't just hope and pray for performance improvements. They plan for short-term wins, organize accordingly, and implement the plan to make things happen. The whole point is not to maximize short-term results at the expense of the future. The point is to make sure that visible results lend sufficient credibility to the transformation effort.

Q: Sounds obvious. So why doesn't everyone do it?
A: For at least three reasons.

First, people don't plan sufficiently for these wins because they are overwhelmed. Often the urgency rate hasn't been pushed high enough, or the vision isn't clear. As a result, the transformation isn't going well and people are scrambling to somehow set things right. With all the panic, planning for short-term wins doesn't receive sufficient time or attention.

In other cases, people don't even try very hard to produce these wins because they believe you can't produce major change *and* achieve excellent short-term results. Thousands and thousands of managers have been taught that life in organizations is a trade-off between the short run and the long run. In this belief system, you can focus long and take your lumps now or you can do well now and throw the future up for grabs. According to this line of thinking, undertaking a major change program means looking to the long term, which in turn means expecting short-term results to be problematic. Sure, you still need to pay attention to the immediate future, but you can't plan for great results. It's just not possible.

Ten years ago I might have agreed with this point of view. But I've seen too much recent evidence that contradicts it. In the words of a renowned executive: "The job of management is to win in the short term while making sure you're in an even stronger position to win in the future." In the past decade, I've watched dozens of firms have it both ways. They transformed themselves into better organizations for the future and they produced good results quarter by quarter.

A third element that undermines the planning for necessary

wins is lack of sufficient management, especially on the guiding coalition, or a lack of commitment by key managers to the change process. To a large degree, leadership deals with the long term and management with the immediate future. Without enough good management, the planning, organizing, and controlling for results will not be sufficient.

Without competent management, inadequate thought is usually given to the whole question of measurement. So existing information systems either fail to record important performance improvements or underestimate their size. Without competent management, tactical choices are glossed over or implemented poorly. Acquisitions are made more on the basis of impulse instead of rational support of the vision. Sequencing of events—do we do the restructuring this year or after the quality effort is farther along—doesn't get sufficient attention.

Because of all of the emphasis on management in the twentieth century, most organizations—with the exception of small, young firms—rarely lack this perspective. Up to a point, small firms can get away without much planning or control. If the company founder is a visionary who dislikes structure (not an unusual situation), he or she may resist the encroachment of managerial thinking, which can then prove to be a problem in this stage of a change effort.

In larger and older firms, the problem of insufficient management is typically associated with either a new strong leader who ignores his managers or a lack of commitment from those managers to the transformation. The former was true in the case of the charismatic division general manager who eventually lost his job. Deep in his heart, he thought people who kept the current system operating were of limited importance. He'd never actually say that, but you could read it between the lines. So when some of those people tried to advise him about short-term economic matters, he often ignored them.

A lack of commitment to change from managers in big, old organizations is often found when the early stages of a transformation are not handled well. With no sense of urgency, a lack of

key managers on the guiding coalition, the failure to communicate an effective vision well, and little effort put into broad-based
employee empowerment, people in overmanaged and underled
organizations sit on the sidelines during change, especially
managers who could be instrumental in producing needed
short-term results.

More Pressure Isn't All Bad

Targeting short-term wins during a transformation effort does
increase the pressures on people. The argument is sometimes
made that these extra demands are inappropriate. "We've got
enough going on," people say, "without more burdens. Give us a
break."

This way of thinking is not without merit. But more often
than not, I've found that short-term pressure can be a useful way
to keep up the urgency rate. A year or two into a major change
program, with the end still not in sight, people naturally tend to
let up. They begin to think: "If this is going to require four more
years, a slide to four and a quarter won't hurt." But as soon as
the urgency rate goes down, everything becomes much harder
to accomplish. Minor tasks that were completed in a month suddenly take three times as long.

Of course, pressure doesn't always produce urgency. The bur-
den of producing short-term wins can create only stress and
exhaustion. In successful change efforts, executives link pressure to urgency through the constant articulation of vision and
strategies. "This is what we are trying to do and this is why it is
so important. Without these short-term wins, we could lose
everything. All that we want to do for our customers, shareholders, employees, and communities becomes problematic. So
we have got to produce these results." This kind of communication gives meaning to hardships and spurs people on. Twelve to
thirty-six months into a major change effort, tired employees
often need renewed motivation.

SHORT-TERM WINS AREN'T SHORT-TERM GIMMICKS

To some degree, all management is manipulation—and that includes the production of short-term performance improvements. But in a few cases I've seen this manipulation taken to new heights, with increased potential for both good and harm.

To keep momentum building in a massive change effort, Phil becomes an accounting magician. He amortizes this, depreciates that, squeezes this group hard, and sells off a few assets. The net result is a bottom line that goes up slowly but steadily each quarter. Anytime people criticize his change program, he thrusts the net income data in their faces much as a fearless vampire killer uses a cross. And the strategy works, at least for a while.

Accounting wizardry of this sort can be helpful in certain difficult situations. But the risks involved are substantial. First, it can be addictive. Once you start this game, stopping can be difficult. Short-term gimmicks can produce problems in the future that often can be covered up only with more short-term gimmicks. Second, it can create more cynics and resisters among the key executives who are sophisticated enough to see what is really happening. Powerful cynics can be very disruptive. Third, it can alienate people who see the practice as unethical.

Some of the downside risk can be eliminated if the entire guiding coalition discusses and agrees to the use of these methods. But even then, contrived results rarely provide a strong enough base on which to build further change in stages 7 and 8. Short-term wins that support transformation are usually genuine. They aren't the product of smoke and mirrors.

THE ROLE OF MANAGEMENT

Systematically targeting objectives and budgeting for them, creating plans to achieve those objectives, organizing for implementation, and then controlling the process to keep it on track—this is the essence of management. With that in mind, one can easily see that the need to create short-term wins in a

EXHIBIT 3

The Relationship of Leadership, Management, Short-Term Results, and Successful Transformation

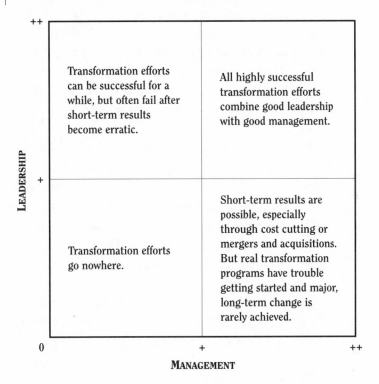

successful change effort demonstrates an important principle: Transformation is not a process involving leadership alone; good management is also essential. A balance of the two is required, as shown in exhibit 3 above.

Because leaders are so central to any major change effort, we sometimes conclude that transformation equals leadership. Certainly without strong and capable leadership from many people, restructurings, turnarounds, and cultural changes don't happen well or at all. But more is involved. Restructuring usually calls for financial expertise, reengineering for technical knowledge, acquisitions for strategic insight. And the process in all major change projects must be managed to keep the operation from lurching out of control or off a cliff.

Q: But isn't the need for management kind of obvious?

A: Generally, yes, but not necessarily to the type of charismatic leaders who sometimes launch transformations.

Charismatic leaders are often poor managers, yet they have a way of convincing us that all we need to do is follow them. "Don't worry about the mundane details; just keep the vision in mind." "Don't concern yourself much with the financials; they will work out fine long term." Our intellect is usually skeptical of this kind of approach, but our hearts can be won over nevertheless.

I'm not suggesting that charisma is bad. The best evidence says that personal appeal can be extremely helpful in a change effort. But when a charismatic leader is not a good manager and doesn't value management skill in others, achieving short-term wins will be problematic at best. As a result, the credibility and momentum typically required to complete stage 7 of a successful transformation are rarely present. As we will see in the next chapter, the magnitude of change in stage 7 is often huge. Alterations of that scale and scope are never made without a solid foundation of credibility and powerful movement forward.

In a way, the primary purpose of the first six phases of the transformation process is to build up sufficient momentum to blast through the dysfunctional granite walls found in so many organizations. When we ignore any of these steps, we put all our efforts at risk.

In enterprises that have been around for decades, the granite walls can be thick. Sometimes, extremely thick.

Consolidating Gains and Producing More Change

➤ | **W**HEN PEOPLE REGISTERED FOR
the annual management meeting,
they were given a packet of materials that included a compilation
of favorable press clippings from
the prior twelve months. At the
opening banquet, the CEO praised
the 110 executives for all they had
accomplished and ended the night
with four toasts. During the first
full day of the meeting, no fewer
than six speakers identified recent
achievements and saluted the
audience. That night, an awards
banquet gave plaques to fifteen
people. The next morning, presentations on "best practices" dis-
solved into more back patting. In
the evening, a famous singer
entertained the group. If all that
didn't send egos into deep space,
the final congratulatory speech by
the CEO did.

Whatever sense of urgency that
had existed at the senior manage-

131

ment level died at that meeting. The implicit message was loud and clear. We can handle this tough market environment. Piece of cake. Look at all we've accomplished recently. We're in great shape. So relax and enjoy the music.

Of course no one actually said, "Relax," and the CEO was very much aware that much more was required to complete a transformation started a few years earlier. All he was trying to do was thank his executives and motivate them with sincere praise. But the message received by the audience was that the difficult work of change was behind them.

During the next year, a dozen change initiatives at that firm were put on hold or slowed down. A consultant's recommendation for a major reorganization in one division was shelved. The third phase in a reengineering effort in another division was temporarily delayed. Suddenly people began having second thoughts about agreed-on alterations in corporate personnel practices. The investment bankers who were trying to divest one business were told to take a rest. Issues identified earlier and marked for action during that year were mostly ignored. By the time key change agents in top management fully realized what was happening, much of the momentum built up after three years of hard work was lost.

Major change often takes a long time, especially in big organizations. Many forces can stall the process far short of the finish line: turnover of key change agents, sheer exhaustion on the part of leaders, bad luck. Under these circumstances, short-term wins are essential to keep momentum going, but the celebration of those wins can be lethal if urgency is lost. With complacency up, the forces of tradition can sweep back in with remarkable force and speed.

RESISTANCE: ALWAYS WAITING TO REASSERT ITSELF

Irrational and political resistance to change never fully dissipates. Even if you're successful in the early stages of a transformation, you often don't win over the self-centered manager who is appalled when a reorganization encroaches on his turf, or the narrowly focused engineer who can't fathom why you want to spend so much time worrying about customers, or the stone-hearted finance executive who thinks empowering employees is ridiculous. You can drive these people underground or into the tall grass. But instead of changing or leaving, they will often sit there waiting for an opportunity to make a comeback. In celebrating short-term wins, change agents can give the opposition just that opportunity.

Sometimes the resisters actually organize the celebration, especially if they are shrewd and cynical. After a hyperventilated meeting, they give voice to the implicit message. I guess that proves we have won, they say. The sacrifices were significant, but we did accomplish something. Now let's all take a deserved breather. If people really are weary, they will be inclined to listen, even if they know that much has yet to be done. They rationalize that a little rest and stability won't hurt. Maybe a vacation will put us in better shape for the next phase.

The consequences of a mistake here can be extremely serious. After watching dozens of major change efforts in the past decade, I'm confident of one cardinal rule: *Whenever you let up before the job is done, critical momentum can be lost and regression may follow.* Until changed practices attain a new equilibrium and have been driven into the culture, they can be very fragile. Three years of work can come undone with remarkable speed. Once regression begins, rebuilding momentum can be a daunting task, not unlike asking people to throw their bodies in front of a huge boulder that has already begun to roll back down the hill. All but change zealots will recoil from this request. Under these circumstances, the human capacity to rationalize is amazing: "I've done my share; now it's Juan's turn." "Maybe we went too far; maybe a little regression is good."

Progress can slip quickly for two reasons. One has to do with corporate culture, and I'll talk more about that in the next chapter. The second is directly related to the kind of increased interdependence that is created by a fast-moving environment, interconnections that make it difficult to change anything without changing everything.

THE PROBLEM OF INTERDEPENDENCE

All organizations are made up of interdependent parts. What happens in the sales department has some effect on the manufacturing group. R&D's work influences product development. Engineering specifications affect manufacturing. The amount of interdependence, however, can vary greatly among organizations depending on a number of factors, none of which is more important than the competitiveness of the business environment.

In the kind of benign oligopolistic world that existed in many major industries for much of the twentieth century, the relatively stable and prosperous environment allowed organizations to minimize internal interdependence. Large in-process inventories buffered various sections of a plant and provided each with some autonomy. Large finished-goods inventories protected manufacturing from actions in the sales department. A slow and linear product development process allowed engineering, sales, marketing, and manufacturing some degree of independence. The lack of better transportation and communication options gave the Malaysian operation considerable freedom from headquarters in New York.

This way of running a business is disappearing for a number of reasons, particularly because of increased competition. With the exception of a few monopolies, organizations cannot now afford big inventories, slow and linear product development, and a foreign operation that goes its own way. Now and in the foreseeable future, most organizations need to be faster, less costly, and more customer focused. As a result, internal interdependencies will grow. Firms are finding that without big inventories, the various parts of a plant need to be much more carefully coordinated, that with pressure to bring out new products faster, the elements of product development need much closer integration, and so on. But these new interconnections greatly complicate transformation efforts, because change happens much more easily in a system of independent parts.

Imagine walking into an office and not liking the way it is

arranged. So you move one chair to the left. You put a few books on the credenza. You get a hammer and rehang a painting. All this may take an hour at most, since the task is relatively straightforward. Indeed, creating change in any system of independent parts is usually not difficult.

Now imagine going into another office where a series of ropes, big rubber bands, and steel cables connect the objects to one another. First, you'd have trouble even walking into the room without getting tangled up. After making your way slowly over to the chair, you try to move it, but find that this lightweight piece of furniture won't budge. Straining harder, you do move the chair a few inches, but then you notice that a dozen books have been pulled off the bookshelf and that the sofa has also moved slightly in a direction you don't like. You slowly work your way over to the sofa and try to push it back into the right spot, which turns out to be incredibly difficult. After thirty minutes, you succeed, but now a lamp has been pulled off the edge of the desk and is precariously hanging in midair, supported by a cable going in one direction and a rope going in the other.

Organizations are coming to look more and more like this bizarre office. Few things move easily, because nearly every element is connected to many other elements. You ask Mary to do something in a new way. Nothing happens. You ask again. She budges an inch. You put pressure on her. Maybe you get two inches. You become furious at Mary, making all sorts of unkind inferences about her character and motivation. But the main problem is that, just like the chair and sofa, a dozen different forces are holding Mary's behavior in place. In her case, instead of ropes and cables and rubber bands you find supervisors, organizational structures, performance appraisal systems, personal habits, cultures, peer relationships, and (most important) an ongoing stream of demands from this group and that department and those people.

Under these circumstances, convincing Mary to behave in new ways can be very difficult. Getting a thousand more employees like her to approach their work differently can be a monumental undertaking.

THE NATURE OF CHANGE IN HIGHLY INTERDEPENDENT SYSTEMS

Most of our direct personal experience with successful change is like the first, real-life office example. The chair isn't in the right place, so we move it. Few if any of us grew up learning how to introduce major change in highly interdependent systems. That, in turn, makes the challenge in organizations today more difficult.

Without much experience, we often don't adequately appreciate a crucial fact: that changing highly interdependent settings is extremely difficult because, ultimately, you have to change nearly everything (see exhibit 1 on the facing page). Because of all the interconnections, you can rarely move just one element by itself. You have to move dozens or hundreds or thousands of elements, which is difficult and time consuming and can rarely if ever be accomplished by just a few people.

Even in the relatively simple case of the interconnected office, interdependencies can seriously complicate change. For example: Let's say we want to make some shifts in a dozen of those offices so the spaces will be more pleasant for visiting customers. We're going to move lamps closer to sofas so clients can read brochures more easily. We're going to switch the chair behind the desk with the less comfortable chair that sits beside the sofas. We're going to take a few pieces of written material that customers always want to see and put them on the coffee tables in front of the sofas. In a dozen real-life offices, where everything is pretty much independent, these changes could be made by one person in an hour or two. In offices strung with ropes, cables, and rubber bands, these changes would require much more time and effort.

So what do you do? If you haven't had much experience with this kind of situation, you'll go find one or two others, ask or order them to help, and then go to work. But after a few frustrating hours in which little is accomplished, your helpers will be looking for any possible excuse to jump ship. Word will then spread quickly about your little change project. Someone who is

---

EXHIBIT 1
Creating Change in Systems of Varying Interdependence

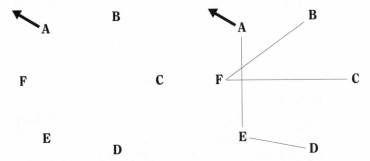

In a system with independent parts, A can be moved by simply moving A.

In a system with some inter-dependence, several elements (A, E, D) may need to be changed in order to move A.

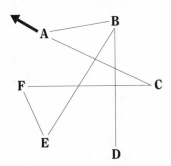

In a system with much inter-dependence, all the elements may need to be changed in order to move A.

zealous about helping customers may volunteer to help. But most people will dive for cover when they see you coming down the hall.

If you've had experience with this kind of change, you'll know that you need to slow down at first to build up the capacity to deal successfully with the situation. Your initial question will be: Is the urgency rate, especially around the issue of helping customers, high enough around here? If the honest answer, confirmed by external sources, is yes, you move ahead. If the answer is no, then the question becomes: How can I reduce complacency and increase urgency?

If you haven't had a lot of experience with changing interdependent systems, you'll probably become pretty impatient pretty fast. "This is ridiculous," you'll say. "I could spend days or weeks trying to push urgency up among this crowd. I don't have that kind of time." So you grab two people and start ordering them to. . . .

Experienced change agents know how to direct their impatience. In this situation, soon after beginning to work on complacency regarding customers, they might take the first steps in putting together a team to guide the project. If the urgency level is at rock bottom, even that won't be possible, because no one will sign up to help. So they may begin trying to clarify the vision of the new office space, all the time placing first priority on lowering complacency.

In this simple case, you may need only one or two other people for your change coalition. The three of you will clarify the overall vision for the effort and calculate strategies for bringing it to life. You'll find ways to communicate this information to the 20 or 50 or 100 other people who have some stake in the situation and its outcome. You'll identify those factors that will hamper implementation of the vision and try to deal with the more serious items on the list. And then, and only then, you'll begin to put together a plan for moving the furniture, to enlist help, and to start working on the offices.

Because this change project is relatively small, indeed trivial compared with retooling a big company, all this activity may take only a few weeks (unless complacency is very high). But to any of your colleagues who have had little experience introducing major change to highly interdependent systems and who have the impulse to grab two others and finish the job in one afternoon, the few weeks of activity will seem like a long time.

Once you get started on the room, you'll probably proceed in a series of projects, not just one big move. You'll discover some sequencing issues; you can't move the desk chair until you first do something else. If you're smart, you'll program in a few short-term wins to keep up group morale. Even with the wins, halfway through this little effort some people will begin to wonder if these changes are really necessary. Surely customers can read without the extra light. The chair by the sofa isn't so bad. Customers can walk; let them go over to the bookcase themselves and get the written material.

If you're really dedicated to fixing up the rooms, you'll find a number of methods to keep the process going. You'll locate a few people who are good at moving furniture in this kind of situation and bring them on board. You'll find newly relevant ways to talk about the overall purpose of the activity so that the communication of the vision doesn't grow stale.

If you don't give up, you'll probably add other projects later in the effort. As you get more and more familiar with all the cables and ropes, you'll discover that some of them seem to serve no useful purpose, and you'll try to get rid of them. Most of the ropes and rubber bands may go easily. The wire cables will prove to be more difficult. You'll also begin to have additional ideas about how you can make life even better for visiting customers. Why not lower the blinds a bit to keep the sun out of their eyes? Instead of making new projects out of each of these ideas, you'll find opportunistic ways to address the issues within currently planned work. Sometimes you'll be successful, sometimes not.

The net effect: You'll end up making more changes than you imagined at first. The entire effort will take more time and energy than you initially expected. One piece of good news is that you'll probably be in a better position to do something similar in the future, because you have both acquired skills and disconnected some of the useless wires and cables. And, of course, in the end, the office will be more customer friendly.

ORGANIZATIONAL TRANSFORMATIONS

The process of introducing change to an organization is not that different from rearranging the furniture in that group of offices. A lot of people need to help. You never have a complete sense of all the changes at the beginning. The warm-up steps take a surprising amount of time and energy. The action eventually occurs in a series of projects. As the magnitude of the effort becomes clear, you will be tempted to give up. If you stay the course, the total time involved will be lengthy.

The first major performance improvement will probably come well before the halfway point. Although some people will want to quit then, in successful transformations the guiding coalition uses the credibility afforded by the short-term win to push forward faster, tackling even more or bigger projects. The restructuring that was avoided early on because of all the resistance is finally undertaken. Two new reengineering projects, both of which were conceived at the beginning of the transformation, are launched. A total reworking of the strategic planning process is finally scheduled. But to restructure, reengineer, and change strategic planning, you find that you also have to alter training programs, modify information systems, add or subtract staff, and introduce new performance appraisal systems. Before long, dozens of elements in the interdependent whole are targeted for action.

People raised in managerial positions during the 1950s and 1960s often can't imagine how ten or twenty change projects can exist simultaneously. But that is precisely what happens in stage 7 of a major transformation.

Q: How can executives manage twenty change projects all at once?

A: They can't. In successful transformations, executives lead the overall effort and leave most of the managerial work and the leadership of specific activities to their subordinates.

Firms that try to juggle twenty change projects today by using the methods that successful companies applied to the same problem three decades ago always seem to fail. No matter how good the people involved, the process simply does not work. Executives end up with sixteen-hour days in endless meetings trying to deal with conflicts and coordination problems, yet even that doesn't overcome a constant string of delays.

The process fails for two interrelated sets of reasons. First, the management approach back then was usually too centralized to handle twenty complex change projects. If a few senior managers try to get involved in all the details, as was often the practice then, everything slows to a crawl. Second, without the guiding vision and alignment that only leadership can provide, the people in charge of each of the projects wind up spending endless hours trying to coordinate their efforts so that they aren't constantly stepping on each other's toes.

Running twenty change projects simultaneously is possible if (a) senior executives focus mostly on the overall leadership tasks and (b) senior executives delegate responsibility for management and more detailed leadership as low as possible in the organization. In this approach, not ten (or a hundred) but a hundred (or a thousand) people are available to help with the twenty projects. More important, the leadership provided by senior executives helps give those other people the information they need to help coordinate their activities without endless planning and meetings.

Imagine two situations. In the first, competent leadership is lacking at the top, and as a result the people trying to run change projects haven't a clue as to what the organization's overall vision is or how their projects fit into that vision. They know only that they are supposed to cut costs in engineering overhead by 20 percent, or reengineer the way parts come into the plant, or redesign the succession planning process. As they try to complete their projects, they find themselves constantly in conflict with two dozen other efforts. No, you can't do it that way, they are told, because that will screw us up. No, I need those resources today; why didn't you inform me about your plans weeks ago? Senior managers try to mediate all the conflicts and set rational priorities, but they simply do not have the time. All this leads to frustration, a growing number of meetings, a political tug of war, and eventually some degree of chaos.

In the second situation, good leadership from above helps everyone understand the big picture, the overall vision and strategies, and the way each project fits into the whole. Here the people working on different activities all aim for the same long-term goal without ever having to meet much. They can also anticipate where conflicts with the other projects might develop, where the priorities should be in light of the overall vision, and what they should do to help move the company forward. Within this framework, conflicts are managed at lower levels in the organization by people who have the time and relevant information. With good leadership from above, these lower-level managers will also be committed to the overall transformation and will thus do what is right with a minimum of parochial political silliness.

With sufficient leadership from above and lots of delegation of both management and leadership activities, twenty change projects can be run simultaneously. If either element is missing, those twenty projects will create chaos, and stage 7 of a major transformation may collapse.

ELIMINATION OF UNNECESSARY INTERDEPENDENCIES

Because internal interconnections make change so difficult, somewhere during this stage of a major transformation effort people begin to raise questions about the need for all the interdependence. They ask: Why should the plant manager have to send report K2A to the finance people at corporate headquarters once a month? Does finance really need that data? Do they need it monthly? Does the plant have to create the report? Why do divisions have to check with corporate HR before making any job offer over $50,000? Does corporate HR need to be involved? If a legitimate reason exists, is $50,000 too low a cutoff point?

This kind of questioning usually escalates when people become angry at the difficulty of producing needed change in highly interdependent systems. If channeled properly, these inquiries can be extremely helpful. All organizations have some unnecessary interdependencies that are the product of history instead of the current reality. Sales can't do something without manufacturing's approval because of a crisis that occurred in 1954, which led to that policy. Cleaning up historical artifacts does create an even longer change agenda, which an exhausted organization will not like. But the purging of unnecessary interconnections can ultimately make a transformation much easier.

EXHIBIT 2
What Stage 7 Looks Like in a Successful, Major Change Effort

➤ *More change, not less:* The guiding coalition uses the credibility afforded by short-term wins to tackle additional and bigger change projects.

➤ *More help:* Additional people are brought in, promoted, and developed to help with all the changes.

➤ *Leadership from senior management:* Senior people focus on maintaining clarity of shared purpose for the overall effort and keeping urgency levels up.

➤ *Project management and leadership from below:* Lower ranks in the hierarchy both provide leadership for specific projects and manage those projects.

➤ *Reduction of unnecessary interdependencies:* To make change easier in both the short and long term, managers identify unnecessary interdependencies and eliminate them.

And in a world where change is increasingly the norm rather than the exception, cleaning house can also make all future reorganizing efforts or strategic shifts less difficult.

A LONG ROAD

Because changing anything of significance in highly interdependent systems often means changing nearly everything, business transformation can become a huge exercise that plays itself out over years, not months. At the extreme, stage 7 can become a decade-long process in which hundreds or thousands of people help lead and manage dozens of change projects. The qualities characterizing stage 7 are listed in exhibit 2 above.

Here, again, is where leadership is invaluable. Outstanding leaders are willing to think long term. Decades or even centuries can be meaningful time frames. Driven by compelling visions that they find personally relevant, they are willing to stay the course to accomplish objectives that are often psychologically important to them. While others shift jobs every two years, leaders will sit in a junior position for twice as long or in a senior position for more than a decade. Instead of declaring victory and giving up or moving on, they will launch the dozen change projects often required in stage 7 of a transformation. They will also take the time to ensure that all the new practices are firmly grounded in the organization's culture.

Because of the nature of management processes, managers often think in terms of much shorter time frames. For them, the short term is this week, the medium term a few months, the long term a year. With that time horizon, announcing victory and stopping change after twenty-four or thirty-six months seems logical. To people who have had a managerial mindset pounded into them for decades, three years can seem like a very, very long time.

Again: Without sufficient leadership, change stalls, and excelling in a rapidly changing world becomes problematic.

CHAPTER 10

Anchoring New Approaches in the Culture

AFTER YEARS OF WORK, THE results were impressive. A once inwardly focused and sluggish aerospace organization was now producing innovative new products at a rapid pace. Not all the offerings were winning in the marketplace, but enough were succeeding that over a five-year period divisional revenues had gone up 62 percent, while net income rose 76 percent; comparable figures for the previous five years were 21 percent and 15 percent, respectively. The division general manager retired, proud that he had helped make an important contribution to the business. He could have stayed a few more years but chose not to: The changes had been made, the results were impressive, the work was done.

At the time of the GM's departure, I don't think anyone fully realized that the new style of operating had never been firmly grounded in the division's culture. If people did, they judged it to be a minor problem. After all, they would say, look at all the change. And look at the results.

Within two years of his retirement, both the new product introduction rate and the success of those products in the marketplace dropped precipitously. Nothing happened suddenly; the regression was all very incremental. At first, no one seemed to notice. After a year, the only top executive who expressed much alarm was a recent arrival from outside the company. Other top executives mostly ignored him.

Here is my postmortem. Some central precepts in the division's culture were incompatible with all the changes that had been made. Yet that inconsistency was never confronted. As long as the division GM and the transformation program worked day and night to reinforce the new practices, the total weight of these efforts overwhelmed the cultural influence. But when the division GM left and the transformation program ended, the culture reasserted itself.

The primary shared value in that organization, a value firmly established in the business's early years, was "developing our technology will solve all problems." Like so much of corporate culture, this idea was never formally stated or written down. When confronted with the belief, most people would readily admit it wasn't entirely true. But give a group of managers three or four beers and then listen to what they had to say, and you heard a lot that sounded like "developing our technology will solve all problems."

Because this core value wasn't diametrically in conflict with the change effort, the two coexisted, although uncomfortably. New practices forced attention first and foremost on customers. The core value would direct it to technology. The new practices were aimed at helping the firm move faster than competitors. The core value said to move at a pace dictated by rational internal technological development.

Someone sensitive to culture would have seen this tension in the company. But because the conflict was so subtle, most people wouldn't have noticed anything. The communication of the vision, the reinforcement by management, the altered performance appraisal, and other influences strongly supported the new practices. You would have had to listen very closely to hear the underlying culture trying to assert itself: "Yes, but, blah-blah blah-blah, technology, blah-blah blah-blah."

Because no one confronted this problem, little if any effort was made to help the new practices grow deep roots, ones that sank down into the core culture or were strong enough to replace it. Shallow roots require constant watering. As long as the GM and other change agents were there daily with the garden hose, all was well. Without that attention, the practices dried up, withered, and died. Other greenery that had been cut back, but that had deeper roots, took over.

Within six months of the division GM's retirement, managers began to more frequently raise questions about business priorities and management practices. Evidence of technological inferiority was nonexistent, yet people said: "I'm afraid that we have been neglecting our technology. If we do that too long, we'll really be in trouble." Meetings among engineers, marketing personnel, sales personnel, and customers became controversial. "The engineers are spending so much time in committees outside their work groups, they're losing their edge." A competitor that ranked seventh in a group of ten on most performance measures suddenly became a standard for comparison. "I recently heard that they spend nearly 20 percent more than we do per employee on R&D. We've got to do something about this."

Within twelve months of the GM's retirement, dozens of little adjustments had been made in how the organization conducted business. Few of those changes were explicitly discussed and affirmed by top management. But the senior executives, with the notable exception of the recent hire, gave tacit approval. Within twenty-four months, some practices regressed to where they had been four years before. Shortly thereafter, the first major performance problems began to emerge.

WHY CULTURE IS POWERFUL

Q: How could an intelligent group of top executives allow something like that to happen?

A: Because their electrical engineering educations, their MBA programs, and their corporate mentors didn't teach them much about organizational culture, especially its powerful influence on behavior. Living in an overmanaged and under-led company for most of their careers just reinforced this blind spot, because culture (and vision) tends to be more the province of leadership, just as structure (and systems) is more of a management tool.

Culture refers to norms of behavior and shared values among a group of people. *Norms of behavior* are common or pervasive ways of acting that are found in a group and that persist because group members tend to behave in ways that teach these practices to new members, rewarding those who fit in and sanctioning those who do not. *Shared values* are important concerns and goals shared by most of the people in a group that tend to shape group behavior and that often persist over time even when group membership changes.

In a big company, one typically finds that some of these social forces—the so-called corporate culture—affect everyone and that others are specific to subunits (for example, the marketing culture, the Detroit office's culture). Regardless of level or location, culture is important because it can powerfully influence human behavior, because it can be difficult to change, and because its near invisibility makes it hard to address directly. Generally, shared values, which are less apparent but more deeply ingrained in the culture, are more difficult to change than norms of behavior. (See exhibit 1 on the facing page.)

When the new practices made in a transformation effort are not compatible with the relevant cultures, they will always be subject to regression. Changes in a work group, a division, or an entire company can come undone, even after years of effort, because the new approaches haven't been anchored firmly in group norms and values.

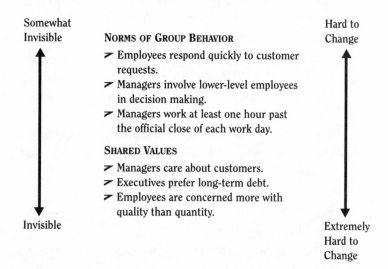

EXHIBIT 1
Components of Corporate Culture: Some Examples

Somewhat
Invisible   **NORMS OF GROUP BEHAVIOR**

➤ Employees respond quickly to customer requests.

➤ Managers involve lower-level employees in decision making.

➤ Managers work at least one hour past the official close of each work day.

SHARED VALUES

➤ Managers care about customers.

➤ Executives prefer long-term debt.

➤ Employees are concerned more with quality than quantity.

Invisible

Hard to Change

Extremely Hard to Change

SOURCE: From *Corporate Culture and Performance* by John P. Kotter and James L. Heskett. Copyright © 1992 by Kotter Associates, Inc. and James L. Heskett. Adapted with permission of The Free Press, a Division of Simon & Schuster.

To understand why culture can be so important, consider this scenario. You graduate from college, apply for jobs, and get three offers. One of the three companies is so enthusiastic about you, and you feel so comfortable with its employees, that you decide to go work there. As a naive twenty-one-year-old, you assume that you have been selected because of your track record, skills, sterling personality, and promise. You also assume you accepted their offer because the company, in an objective sense, was an excellent corporation. You are mostly oblivious to another major screening criteria: culture.

Few if any of the people recruiting you explicitly said: "One of the big reasons we're hiring you is because we think you will fit in, that you share our implicit values and beliefs, and that you will adjust easily to our norms." They probably didn't say this because they are unaware of how strongly they apply cultural criteria in hiring. In accepting their offer, you may also have been oblivious to the weight you were putting on value fit. The net result is that you and probably all your recently hired peers are easy candidates for what is called "socialization"—the inculcation of the company's norms and values.

During your first year on the job, you're eager to do well and so are particularly alert to clues about how people are accepted and promoted. As long as those practices don't seem foolish or unethical, you try to adopt them. Often, the biggest lessons don't come in a training session or a manual for new employees. The day your boss goes up in smoke over something you do—that is influential. The day you say something in a meeting and a stony silence comes over the group—that is influential. The day an older secretary pulls you aside and reads you the riot act—that is influential. The net result is that you learn and assimilate the culture.

For the next twenty years, you are promoted once every thirty to fifty months. During this time, the culture becomes more and more an instinctive part of you. Indeed, one of the reasons you've gotten promoted is because you fit in and get along with the people who decide on promotion. After a while, although you may not be aware of it, you are teaching the new hires the culture. Indeed, at age fifty, as a senior-level manager, you may be almost oblivious to the culture. You have lived in it for so long, and found it so compatible from the beginning, that you relate to the culture as a fish does to water. Because it is everywhere yet invisible, you just don't think about it, despite the big influence it has on you. Fish get air and food from the water. You get a certain pleasing predictability, lots of positive reinforcement, and a strong emotional attachment to your organization through its culture.

To a large degree, most of the people of your generation in the firm have had similar experiences. Most of these men and women were selected for cultural compatibility. Most had hundreds or thousands of hours of experience in which the norms and values were taught and reinforced. Most now teach the younger employees.

Culture is powerful for three primary reasons:

1. Because individuals are selected and indoctrinated so well.

2. Because the culture exerts itself through the actions of hundreds or thousands of people.

3. Because all of this happens without much conscious intent and thus is difficult to challenge or even discuss.

Consultants, industrial salespeople, and others who regularly see firms up close without being employees know well how much culture operates outside of people's awareness, even rather visibly unusual aspects of a culture. I can still remember going into a major publishing company about twenty years ago and finding that eight of the top eleven male officers were under 5'8" tall. (The firm's founder was 5'6".) When I commented on that fact in an off-hand remark that certainly wasn't meant to be disapproving, the others in the room looked at me as if I were a space alien. At another big company where the first major product had been an explosive and where safety had been an obsession for more than a century, I found that virtually all executives walked up or down stairwells clutching the handrail as if they were all ninety-nine years old.

Because corporate culture exerts this kind of influence, the new practices created in a reengineering or a restructuring or an acquisition must somehow be anchored in it; if not, they can be very fragile and subject to regression.

WHEN NEW PRACTICES ARE GRAFTED ONTO THE OLD CULTURE

In many transformation efforts, the core of the old culture is not incompatible with the new vision, although some specific norms will be. In that case, the challenge is to graft the new practices onto the old roots while killing off the inconsistent pieces.

For one leading manufacturer of industrial equipment, a "customer-first" attitude had always been at the center of its cul-

ture. During the early years, the practices surrounding this attitude were created by the founder and mimicked by everyone
else. In the middle part of the twentieth century, with the
founder long dead and the firm having a hundred-year history in
helping customers, senior management decided to turn this
knowledge into explicit procedures that could be taught more
easily to an ever-increasing employee base. By 1980, these procedures filled six notebooks, each nearly three inches thick. At
that point, "doing it by the book" was a deeply ingrained habit
and cultural norm.

In 1983, a new CEO put the company through a major transformation process that was successful. By 1988, the old proce-
dure manuals were no longer used, replaced by far fewer rules
and a set of customer-first practices that made more sense in the
1980s. But the CEO realized that the old manuals, while not on
people's desks, were still very much in the corporate culture. So
here is what he did.

When he took the stage for his keynote address at the annual
management meeting, he had three of his officers stack the old
manuals on a table next to the lectern. In his speech he said
something like this:

> These books served us well for many years. They codified wisdom
> and experience developed over decades and made that available
> to all of us. I'm sure that many thousands of our customers ben-
> efited enormously because of these procedures.
>
> In the past few decades, our industry has changed in some
> important ways. Where there once were only two major com-
> petitors, we now have six. Where a new generation of products
> used to be delivered once every two decades, the time has now
> been cut to nearly five years. Where once customers were
> delighted if they could receive help from us in forty-eight hours,
> they now expect service within the course of an eight-hour shift.
>
> In this new context, our wonderful old books began to show
> their age—they weren't serving customers as well. They didn't
> help us adapt well to changing conditions. They slowed us down.
> The first evidence we saw of this was in the late 1970s. Although
> we continued to try to do the right thing, those buying our prod-

ucts didn't perceive it that way, and it began to show up in our financials.

In 1983, we decided that we had to do something about this—not only because the economic results were looking poor but even more so because we were no longer doing what we wanted to do and had done so well for so long: serve our customers' needs in a truly outstanding way. We reexamined their requirements and in the last three years have changed dozens of practices to meet those needs. And in the process, we set these guys [pointing to the books] aside.

I think at times all of us worried about whether we were doing the right thing. Well, the evidence is pretty clear now.

He went on at length at this point to review customer satisfaction surveys that showed both improved ratings and clear linkages between those ratings and the new practices.

So I think we are living up to our heritage, despite a difficult competitive situation. I'm taking time to tell you all this today for a number of reasons. I know that there are a few of you in this room, each new to the company in the last couple of years, who think the books over here are a joke, bureaucratic mindlessness in the extreme. Well, I want you to know that they served this company well for many years. I also know that there are people in this room who hate to see the books go. You might not admit it—the logical case for what we've done is far too compelling—but at some gut level, you feel that way. I want you to join with me today in saying good-bye. The books are like an old friend who's died after living a good life. We need to acknowledge his contribution to our lives and move on.

The speech, in its totality, took about thirty minutes. The tone was that of a eulogy. Here we see a man trying respectfully to bury an old set of practices while making sure that their replacements are firmly connected to the group's core values. The analytical side of our brains has trouble seeing the need for this. If we were only analytical, such a speech wouldn't be necessary. But human beings are also emotional creatures, and we ignore that reality at our peril.

From all I've seen, that speech and associated follow-up measures have been very successful. An almost kneejerk reaction to "do it by the book," especially among older employees, has been replaced with support for a more sensible set of practices. That's not a small accomplishment.

In the next few decades, I think we'll have to be doing a lot more of this sort of limited cultural modification. The increased globalization of enterprises will present one variation on this problem a million times over. The new Korean (or Russian) subsidiary doesn't have the same customer orientation (or attention to costs) as called for in the corporate vision. The problem is not that the new foreign entity is anticustomer (or anticost), and the solution is not to try to re-create New York in Seoul. The challenge will be to graft some key values onto already well-formed cultures.

Today, I don't think there are many companies that are very good at this kind of activity. We either ignore norms and values or become cultural imperialists, trying to shove our practices in detail down people's throats. In a globalizing economy, most of us will be forced to confront this issue in the not so distant future.

WHEN NEW PRACTICES REPLACE THE OLD CULTURE

Anchoring a new set of practices in a culture is difficult enough when those approaches are consistent with the core of the culture. When they aren't, the challenge can be much greater.

Consider a firm founded in 1928. The key experience that shaped its culture was the Great Depression, and as a result, conservative—if not risk-averse—norms and values permeated the company. When the firm stumbled badly in the late 1980s and a new top management team engineered major changes, the tensions between its take-a-risk practices and the old culture were gigantic. Even after top management communicated 100 percent support for the new methods and the evidence began to accumulate that they were working, the old culture refused to die, especially in one part of the company.

What did these managers do? Briefly:

1. They talked a great deal about the evidence showing how per-formance improvements were linked to their new practices.

2. They talked a great deal about where the old culture had come from, how it had served the firm well, but why it was no longer helpful.

3. They offered those over fifty-five an attractive early retire-ment program and then worked hard to convince anyone who embraced the new culture not to leave.

4. They made doubly sure that new hires were not being infor-mally screened according to the old norms and values.

5. They tried hard not to promote anyone who didn't viscerally appreciate the new practices.

6. They made sure that the three candidates being considered to replace the CEO had none of the Depression-era culture in their hearts.

Even with all of these efforts, killing off the old culture and cre-ating the new one was difficult to accomplish. Shared values and group norms are persistent, especially the former (see exhibit 1 on page 149). When shared values are supported by the hiring of similar personalities into an organization, changing the culture may require changing people. Even when there is no personali-ty incompatibility with a new vision, if shared values are the product of many years of experience in a firm, years of a differ-ent kind of experience are often needed to create any change.

And that is why cultural change comes at the end of a trans-formation, not the beginning.

CULTURAL CHANGE COMES LAST, NOT FIRST

One of the theories about change that has circulated widely over the past fifteen years might be summarized as follows: The biggest impediment to creating change in a group is culture.

Therefore, the first step in a major transformation is to alter the norms and values. After the culture has been shifted, the rest of the change effort becomes more feasible and easier to put into effect.

I once believed in this model. But everything I've seen over the past decade tells me it's wrong.

Culture is not something that you manipulate easily. Attempts to grab it and twist it into a new shape never work because you can't grab it. Culture changes only after you have successfully altered people's actions, after the new behavior produces some group benefit for a period of time, and after people see the connection between the new actions and the performance improvement. Thus, most cultural change happens in stage 8, not stage 1.

This does not mean that a sensitivity to cultural issues isn't essential in the first phases of a transformation. The better you understand the existing culture, the more easily you can figure out how to push the urgency level up, how to create the guiding coalition, how to shape the vision, and so forth. Nor does this mean that changing behavior isn't a key part of the early stages of a transformation. In step 2, for example, you are typically trying to alter habits and create more teamwork among a guiding coalition. Nor does this mean that some attitudinal changes are not a part of step 1, where complacent worldviews are attacked. But the actual changing of powerful norms and values occurs mostly in the very last stage of the process, or at least the very last stage in each cycle of the process. So if one of the change cycles in a larger transformation effort is associated with a reengineering project in department X, that project will end with an effort to anchor the work in the department's culture.

A good rule of thumb: *Whenever you hear of a major restructuring, reengineering, or strategic redirection in which step 1 is "changing the culture," you should be concerned that it might be going down the wrong path.*

Both attitude and behavior change typically begin early in a transformation process. These alterations then create changes in practices that help a firm produce better products or services

---

EXHIBIT 2
Anchoring Change in a Culture

➤ *Comes last, not first:* Most alterations in norms and shared values come at the end of the transformation process.

➤ *Depends on results:* New approaches usually sink into a culture only after it's very clear that they work and are superior to old methods.

➤ *Requires a lot of talk:* Without verbal instruction and support, people are often reluctant to admit the validity of new practices.

➤ *May involve turnover:* Sometimes the only way to change a culture is to change key people.

➤ *Makes decisions on succession crucial:* If promotion processes are not changed to be compatible with the new practices, the old culture will reassert itself.

at lower costs. But only at the end of the change cycle does most of this become anchored in the culture.

I've seen a dozen cases over the past decade in which the senior VPs of human resources were assigned to "change the culture" in firms with no overall transformation process or in firms with a project that was run independently or ahead of bigger change efforts. Typically, these HR managers struggled along for a few years trying hard to do something useful. They would produce statements of desired values or group norms. They would hold meetings to communicate this information. Sometimes they would launch training programs to "teach" the values. But as staff executives, they were in a weak position to introduce a major change that would affect the entire organization. And the basic conception of the proposal—to get in there and hammer that culture into shape—made success virtually impossible from the outset.

Some observers are dismissive of these cases and the people associated with them. But I've found these executives are usually smart, dedicated, and hard-working individuals. Their failures tell us less about them than about the extraordinary difficulty of changing corporate culture. (See exhibit 2 on page 157, which sums up the key features of anchoring cultural change.)

It is because such change is so difficult to bring about that the transformation process has eight stages instead of two or three, that it often takes so much time, and that it requires so much leadership from so many people.

PART III

Implications for the Twenty-first Century

CHAPTER 11

The Organization of the Future

➤ | THE RATE OF CHANGE IN THE business world is not going to slow down anytime soon. If anything, competition in most industries will probably speed up over the next few decades. Enterprises everywhere will be presented with even more terrible hazards and wonderful opportunities, driven by the globalization of the economy along with related technological and social trends.

The typical twentieth-century organization has not operated well in a rapidly changing environment. Structure, systems, practices, and culture have often been more of a drag on change than a facilitator. If environmental volatility continues to increase, as most people now predict, the standard organization of the twentieth century will likely become a dinosaur.

So what will the winning

enterprise of the twenty-first century look like? Speculating on the future is always hazardous, but the discussion presented in this book has rather clear implications.

A PERSISTENT SENSE OF URGENCY

Major change is never successful unless the complacency level is low. A high urgency rate helps enormously in completing all the stages of a transformation process. If the rate of external change continues to climb, then the urgency rate of the winning twenty-first-century organization will have to be medium to high all the time. The twentieth-century model of lengthy periods of calm or complacency being punctuated by shorter periods of hectic activity will not work.

A higher rate of urgency does not imply ever present panic, anxiety, or fear. It means a state in which complacency is virtually absent, in which people are always looking for both problems and opportunities, and in which the norm is "do it now."

Keeping urgency up will require, first and foremost, performance information systems that are far superior to what we generally see today. The tradition of distributing financial accounting data to a small number of people on a monthly or quarterly basis will have to become a thing of the past. More people, more often, will need data on customers, competitors, employees, suppliers, shareholders, technological developments, and financial results. The systems that supply this information cannot be designed, as are some today, to make the organization or one of its units look good. They will need to be created to provide honest and unvarnished news, especially about performance.

In the past decade, a number of firms have taken important steps toward creating these new performance feedback systems. Information on customer satisfaction, in particular, is being collected more accurately, more often, and for more people. Likewise, managers are actually seeing customers, especially disgruntled ones, more often. All this is good, but we still have a long way to go. Typical employees in typical firms today still receive little data on their performance, the performance of their group or department, and the performance of the firm.

To both create these systems and use their output productively, corporate cultures in the twenty-first century will have to value candid discussions far more than they do today. Norms associated with political politeness, with nonconformational diplomaticese, and with killing-the-messenger-of-bad-news will have to change. The volume knob on the dishonest dialog channel will have to be turned way down.

For those readers who have lived in hopelessly political organizations most of their careers and who therefore think this goal is quixotic, I can only point out that these kinds of candid and honest cultures do exist today. I've seen them. Creating those norms can certainly be difficult, but the task is not impossible. Typically, the change begins with a single powerful person, spreads from him or her to a few others through example, produces some group benefit, and then spreads still more widely.

The combination of valid data from a number of external sources, broad communication of that information inside an organization, and a willingness to deal honestly with the feedback will go a long way toward squashing complacency. An increased sense of urgency, in turn, will help organizations change more easily and better deal with a rapidly changing environment.

TEAMWORK AT THE TOP

In a slow-moving world, all an organization needs is a good executive in charge. Teamwork at the top is not essential. In a moderately paced context, teamwork is necessary to deal with periodic transformations, but much of the time the old model will still work. In a fast-moving world, teamwork is enormously helpful almost all the time.

In an environment of constant change, individuals, even if supremely talented, won't have enough time or expertise to absorb rapidly shifting competitor, customer, and technological information. They won't have enough time to communicate all the important decisions to hundreds or thousands of others. They will rarely have the charisma or skills to singlehandedly gain commitments to change from large numbers of people.

I can imagine a day not long from now when succession at the top of firms may no longer be an exercise in picking one person to replace another. Succession could be a process of picking at least the core of a team. With the basic elements of a sensible team in place on day one, a new CEO would be in a much stronger position to build the kind of coalition needed to handle change. Team building that can take months, if not years, could be replaced with a much shorter process.

I can also imagine a day when big egos and snakes are eliminated from promotion lists, no matter how smart, clever, hard working, or well educated they are. Such people kill teamwork. They create problems today, but in a more rapidly changing future world, the consequences of their actions might well become completely unacceptable.

Neither of these ideas—promoting teams instead of individuals and eliminating gigantic egos and snakes—will ever be accepted without considerable controversy. Succession as a team choice is a radical thought, especially in the United States, with its lone-cowboy tradition. Not promoting smart and talented people is less radical, but the snakes and big egos will not go down without a fight. Imagine the dialogue:

"This is ridiculous. Nick is brilliant and dynamic. What kind of a signal will we be sending to the young people around here if we don't promote him?"

"We are trying to send a signal that caring much more about yourself than the company is unacceptable."

"How can you say that he doesn't care about the company? OK, he's a little self-centered, but most talented people are."

"How come so many people seem to dislike him?"

"Jealousy. All great talents suffer. . . ."

I think I can make the argument that succession decisions will be simpler with this new approach because we will no longer be hunting for the elusive single individual who can jump tall buildings in a single bound. I also think some trends (such as 360-degree performance appraisals) are already taking a toll on snakes and big egos. Still, these changes are controversial, and they won't come about easily.

PEOPLE WHO CAN CREATE AND COMMUNICATE VISION

In the twentieth century, the development of business professionals in the classroom and on the job focused on management—that is, people were taught how to plan, budget, organize, staff, control, and problem solve. Only in the last decade or so has much thought gone into developing leaders—people who can create and communicate visions and strategies. Because management deals mostly with the status quo and leadership deals mostly with change, in the next century we will have to become much more skilled at creating leaders. Without enough leaders, the vision, communication, and empowerment that are at the heart of transformation will simply not happen well enough or fast enough to satisfy our needs and expectations.

Some people believe the task of developing many leaders is hopeless. You're either born with it or you're not, they say, and most people aren't. Even if we accept this pessimistic assumption and say that only one person in a hundred has much leadership potential, with a worldwide population of 5.7 billion, that leaves close to 60 million people with leadership possibilities. Sixty million is a lot of people! If we can help develop that potential, we will have plenty of leadership to guide organizations in a more rapidly changing twenty-first century.

Development of leadership potential doesn't happen in a two-week course or even a four-year college program, although both can help. Most complex skills emerge over decades, which is why we increasingly talk about "lifelong learning." Because we spend so many of our waking hours at work, most of our development takes place—or doesn't take place—on the job. This simple fact has enormous implications. If our time at work encourages and helps us to develop leadership skills, we will eventually realize whatever potential we have. Conversely, if time at work does little or nothing to develop those skills, we will probably never live up to our potential.

Highly controlling organizations often destroy leadership by not allowing people to blossom, test themselves, and grow. In stiff bureaucracies, young men and women with potential typically see few good role models, are not encouraged to lead, and may even be punished if they go out of bounds, challenge the status quo, and take risks. These kinds of organizations tend either to repel people with leadership potential or to take those individuals and teach them only about bureaucratic management.

Successful organizations in the twenty-first century will have to become more like incubators of leadership. Wasting talent will become increasingly costly in a world of rapid change. Developing that leadership will, in turn, demand flatter and leaner structures along with less controlling and more risk-taking cultures. The negative consequences of putting people with potential into small boxes and micromanaging them will only increase. People need to be encouraged to attempt to lead, at first on a small scale, both to help the organization adapt to changing circumstances and to help themselves to grow. In this way, through thousands of hours of trial and error, coaching, and encouragement, they will achieve their potential.

In the last ten years alone, we have come a long way toward creating this kind of organization. Anyone pessimistic about our capacity to build leadership-incubating structures should look carefully at what already has happened. But we still have a long way to go. Narrowly defined jobs, risk-averse cultures, and micromanaging bosses are the norm in far too many places— especially in big companies and many government organizations.

BROAD-BASED EMPOWERMENT

The hearts and minds of all members of the workforce are needed to cope with the fast-shifting realities of the business climate. Without sufficient empowerment, critical information about quality sits unused in workers' minds and energy to implement changes lies dormant.

Many of the same kinds of organizational attributes required to develop leadership are also needed to empower employees. Those facilitating factors would include flatter hierarchies, less bureaucracy, and a greater willingness to take risks. In addition, constant empowerment for a constantly changing world works best in organizations in which senior managers focus on leadership and in which they delegate most managerial responsibilities to lower levels.

Even today, the best-performing firms I know that operate in highly competitive industries have executives who spend most of their time leading, not managing, and employees who are empowered with the authority to manage their work groups. I can't conceive of how the trend in this direction won't continue over the next few decades, despite some resistance from both managers and workers who are attached to the old model.

For readers who have difficulty imagining this degree of empowerment actually emerging in the workplace, I suggest you look at organizations that operate today in a sea of shifting conditions: high-tech companies generally and professional service firms that thrive in intensely competitive environments. What you will find are unusually flat hierarchies, little bureaucracy, a propensity for risk taking, workforces that largely manage themselves, and senior-level people who focus on providing leadership for client projects, technological development, or customer service. The model has already been tested. With proper leadership at the top, it works extremely well.

DELEGATED MANAGEMENT FOR EXCELLENT SHORT-TERM PERFORMANCE

Some business futurists write as if management as we know it will disappear in the twenty-first century. Everyone of importance will become visionary and inspiring. Those boring people who worry about whether inventories are on target will no longer be needed.

But this is unrealistic.

Even in a rapidly changing world, someone has to make the current system perform to expectations or those in power will lose the support of important constituencies. Shooting for a better future is terrific, but if short-term wins don't demonstrate that you're on the right path, you will rarely get the chance to fully implement your vision.

Since the kind of organization we are describing here delegates a great deal of authority to lower levels, excellence in management means that the empowered employees handle this responsibility well. That, in turn, means they must receive sufficient management training and be supported with the appropriate systems. Today, even when you find managerially empowered employees, they often have not been given sufficient educational and other assistance. Instead, both training and systems are still designed to serve the needs of a bloated middle management.

Changing this reality is usually more of an attitudinal challenge than a technical or economic issue. "No, this training is for managers," someone says, meaning that you have to have a certain minimum status in the hierarchy to deserve the educational perk. "We can't give this information out to all those people," someone else says in response to a proposal for shifting the control systems. "Why not?" you ask. They answer:

1. "Because of security." The real question is, whose security? If information on the poor performance of some department or some product is widely known, will this hurt the firm? Or will it embarrass a few executives and put pressure on certain people to do something?

2. "Because they won't know what to do with the information." They will if they've been trained.

3. "Because of the expense." Curious logic. By delegating management responsibility, we're getting people who typically make $20,000 to $50,000 a year to do work that used to be done by people making $50,000 to $200,000 per year. The

payroll savings will always outdistance any training or new system expenses, unless you retain unnecessary middle management jobs.

An organization with more delegation, which means a lean and flat hierarchy, is in a far superior position to maneuver than one with a big, change-resistant lump in the middle. This fact alone will force more delegation over the next few decades, despite all the excuses offered as to why that's a bad idea.

NO UNNECESSARY INTERDEPENDENCE

All organizations have unneeded internal interconnections between people and groups. The German subsidiary can't agree to anything without checking with corporate. The controller's department in the head office sends a hundred pounds of reports per week to the plants, where the paper is largely ignored. Because of some problem back in 1965, a routine was created in which engineers make certain presentations to marketing and manufacturing people, meetings that still go on today despite the existence of information technology that can communicate the same information more quickly and easily. In some firms, this useless interdependence is nearly overwhelming, making major change a hopelessly complicated affair. Although such situations may seem foolish on the outside, on the inside they can be accepted, perhaps grudgingly, and very hard to alter.

In the twenty-first century, a volatile business environment will force more organizations to coordinate their subunits quickly and inexpensively. Interdependencies left over from an earlier era that add no value will be less tolerable. In this sense, the twenty-first-century organization will probably be a lot cleaner than the one we typically see today. Fewer structural cobwebs and less procedural dust will make surfaces slicker and faster.

Furthermore, a process of continual cleaning will certainly be encouraged in a faster-moving environment. Instead of waiting for interdependencies to reach unmanageable levels, the effective organization in the next century will reexamine linkages on a more regular basis and eliminate those that are no longer relevant.

Again, for those who can't quite imagine this scenario, I assure you it's already happening today, although not often. A number of firms I know that are still being run by founders or other entrepreneurs are almost obsessive about keeping interdependencies down to the bare minimum demanded by the market environment. Doing this well isn't easy. Linkages give power to some people who are then often reluctant to give it up. Linkages become habits. Deciding what is a relevant linkage and what is a historical artifact can occasionally be difficult, especially in the absence of a broader vision and strategy guiding the organization. Nevertheless, some people today succeed wonderfully here with obsessive attention to this issue.

AN ADAPTIVE CORPORATE CULTURE

In total, all of the practices I've been describing here will help an organization adapt to a rapidly changing environment. Creating those practices so they stick is an exercise in creating adaptive corporate cultures.

In the twentieth century, we have found group norms and shared values in organizations mostly to be barriers to change. They don't need to be. Cultures can facilitate adaptation if they value performing well for an organization's constituencies, if they really support competent leadership and management, if they encourage teamwork at the top, and if they demand a minimum of layers, bureaucracy, and interdependencies.

Creating such cultures is an exercise in transformation: increasing the urgency rate, creating the guiding coalition, and so on. In most industries today, the pressure to change cultures is not intense, so it's easy to delay. "Let the next generation of executives do it." "Things aren't so bad; look at last quarter's net income."

Keep one fact in mind as you consider this: At least one player in your industry probably isn't thinking that way.

Truly adaptive firms with adaptive cultures are awesome competitive machines. They produce superb products and services faster and better. They run circles around bloated bureaucracies. Even when they have far fewer resources and patents or less market share, they compete and win again and again.

People who have been jerked around in marginally effective restructurings, quality programs, and the like often worry that this ever changing, adaptive organization will be hell on earth. It's not. From what I've seen so far, this type of organization can be a far more fulfilling workplace than is today's norm. Remember, change doesn't happen in this kind of enterprise as a means of satisfying someone's ego or as a knee-jerk reaction to yesterday's events. Changes occur to help make better and better products or services that serve real human needs at lower and lower costs. Living and winning in that environment can be fun, because you feel like you're doing something worthwhile. The pace of change does require getting used to, especially if you have spent most of your work life in old-fashioned bureaucracies. But after a period of adjustment, most people seem to like the dynamic quality of the environment. It's challenging. It's never boring. Winning is fun. And for most of us, making a real contribution is pleasing to the soul.

GETTING FROM HERE TO THERE

I've summarized the discussion in this chapter in exhibit 1 on the following page. Just a glance at that information shows that we are talking about a great deal of rather fundamental change. That much change will not come quickly.

EXHIBIT 1

The Twentieth- and Twenty-first-Century Organization Compared

TWENTIETH CENTURY	TWENTY-FIRST CENTURY
STRUCTURE	STRUCTURE
➤ Bureaucratic	➤ Nonbureaucratic, with fewer rules and employees
➤ Multileveled	➤ Limited to fewer levels
➤ Organized with the expectation that senior management will manage	➤ Organized with the expectation that management will lead, lower-level employees will manage
➤ Characterized by policies and procedures that create many complicated internal interdependencies	➤ Characterized by policies and procedures that produce the minimal internal interdependence needed to serve customers
SYSTEMS	SYSTEMS
➤ Depend on few performance information systems	➤ Depend on many performance information systems, providing data on customers especially
➤ Distribute performance data to executives only	➤ Distribute performance data widely
➤ Offer management training and support systems to senior people only	➤ Offer management training and support systems to many people
CULTURE	CULTURE
➤ Inwardly focused	➤ Externally oriented
➤ Centralized	➤ Empowering
➤ Slow to make decisions	➤ Quick to make decisions
➤ Political	➤ Open and candid
➤ Risk averse	➤ More risk tolerant

The single biggest argument offered against the need for transformation is that organizations can succeed with incremental change. A 2 percent improvement here, a 5 percent cost reduction there, and you win. In the short run, in certain industries, this can be true. But look at the exhibit. How long do you think it will take to move incrementally from the twentieth-century model to the twenty-first?

And what do you think will be the consequences if you don't get there fast enough?

CHAPTER 12

Leadership and Lifelong Learning

➤ THE KEY TO CREATING AND sustaining the kind of successful twenty-first-century organization described in chapter 11 is leadership—not only at the top of the hierarchy, with a capital *L*, but also in a more modest sense (*l*) throughout the enterprise. This means that over the next few decades we will see both a new form of organization emerge to cope with faster-moving and more competitive environments and a new kind of employee, at least in successful firms.

The twenty-first-century employee will need to know more about both leadership and management than did his or her twentieth-century counterpart. The twenty-first-century manager will need to know much about leadership. With these skills, the type of "learning organization" discussed in chapter 11 can be built and maintained. Without these skills, dynamic adaptive enterprises are not possible.

For those raised on traditional notions about leadership, this idea makes no sense. In the most commonly known historical model, leadership is the province of the chosen few. Within that framework, the concept of masses of people helping to provide the leadership needed to drive the eight-stage change process is at best foolhardy. Even if you think you reject the old model, if you have lived on planet earth during the twentieth century this highly elitist notion is likely buried somewhere in your head and may affect your actions in ways invisible to you.

The single biggest error in the traditional model is related to its assumptions about the origins of leadership. Stated simply, the historically dominant concept takes leadership skills as a divine gift of birth, a gift granted to a small number of people. Although I, too, once believed this, I have found that the traditional idea simply does not fit well with what I have observed in nearly thirty years of studying organizations and the people who run them. In particular, the older model is nearly oblivious to the power and the potential of lifelong learning.

A Prototype of the Twenty-first-Century Executive

I first met Manny in 1986. At that time, he was an alert, friendly, and ambitious forty-year-old manager. He had already done well in his career, but nothing about him seemed exceptional. No one in his firm, at least as much as I could tell, called him "a leader." I found him to be a little cautious and somewhat political, like many people raised in twentieth-century bureaucracies. I would have expected him to remain in a senior staff job for a few decades and to make a useful but far from outstanding contribution to his corporation.

The second time I met Manny was in 1995. In only a short conversation, I could sense a depth and sophistication that had been unapparent before. In talking with others at his company, again and again I heard a similar assessment. "Isn't it amazing how much Manny has grown," they told me. "Yes," I said, "it's amazing."

Today Manny is running a business that will generate about $600 million in after-tax profits. That business is rapidly globalizing with all the attendant hazards and opportunities. As I write this, he is leading his group through a major transformation designed to position the organization for a promising future. All from a man who did not look like a leader, much less a great leader, at age forty.

A few people like Manny have always been around. Instead of slowing down and peaking at age thirty-five or forty-five, they keep learning at a rate we normally associate only with children and young adults. These exceptions to the norm help us see that nothing inherent in human DNA prevents growth later in life. The biography that I'm now completing of Japanese industrialist Konosuke Matsushita, one of the twentieth century's most remarkable business leaders, shows this tendency in an extreme form. Descriptions of Matsushita early in life tell us of a hardworking but sickly young man. Nowhere are terms such as *brilliant, dynamic, visionary,* or *charismatic* used to describe him then, much less *leader*. Yet he grew to be an entrepreneur during his twenties, a business leader in his thirties and forties, and a major-league organizational transformer in his fifties. As a result, he helped his firm rebound after the horrors of World War II, absorb new technology, expand globally, and renew itself again and again so as to succeed beyond anyone's dreams. He then took on additional successful careers as a writer in his sixties, a philanthropist in his seventies, and an educator in his eighties.

In the twenty-first century, I think we will see more of these remarkable leaders who develop their skills through lifelong learning, because that pattern of growth is increasingly being rewarded by a rapidly changing environment. In a static world, we can learn virtually everything we need to know in life by the time we are fifteen, and few of us are called on to provide leadership. In an ever changing world, we can never learn it all, even if we keep growing into our nineties, and the development of leadership skills becomes relevant to an ever-increasing number of people.

As the rate of change increases, the willingness and ability to keep developing become central to career success for individuals and to economic success for organizations. People like Manny or Matsushita often do not begin the race with the most money or intelligence, but they win nevertheless because they outgrow their rivals. They develop the capacity to handle a complex and changing business environment. They grow to become unusually competent in advancing organizational transformation. They learn to be leaders.

THE VALUE OF COMPETITIVE CAPACITY

The importance of lifelong learning in an increasingly changing business environment and its relationship to leadership was demonstrated rather dramatically in a twenty-year study of 115 students from the Harvard Business School class of 1974. In attempting to explain why most were doing well in their careers despite the challenging economic climate that took shape at about the time they graduated, I found that two elements stood out: competitive drive and lifelong learning. These factors seemed to give people an edge by creating an unusually strong competitive capacity (see exhibit 1 on the facing page). Competitive drive helped create lifelong learning, which kept increasing skill and knowledge levels, especially leadership skills, which in turn produced a prodigious ability to deal with an increasingly difficult and fast-moving global economy. Like Manny, people with high standards and a strong willingness to learn became measurably stronger and more able leaders at age fifty than they had been at age forty.

Marcel DePaul was typical of this group. He grew up in a middle-class family and attended a good but not outstanding university in Michigan. He was admitted to the MBA program based less on test scores than on an impressive track record both in

EXHIBIT 1

The Relationship of Lifelong Learning, Leadership Skills, and the Capacity to Succeed in the Future

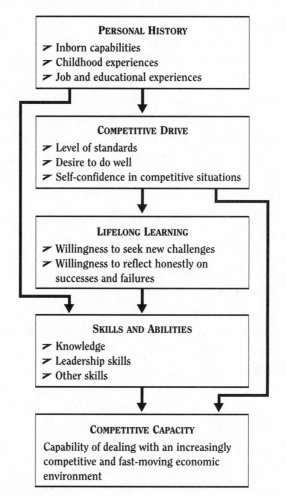

PERSONAL HISTORY
- Inborn capabilities
- Childhood experiences
- Job and educational experiences

COMPETITIVE DRIVE
- Level of standards
- Desire to do well
- Self-confidence in competitive situations

LIFELONG LEARNING
- Willingness to seek new challenges
- Willingness to reflect honestly on successes and failures

SKILLS AND ABILITIES
- Knowledge
- Leadership skills
- Other skills

COMPETITIVE CAPACITY
Capability of dealing with an increasingly competitive and fast-moving economic environment

SOURCE: From *The New Rules: How to Succeed in Today's Post-Corporate World* by John P. Kotter. Copyright © 1995 by John P. Kotter. Adapted with permission of The Free Press, a Division of Simon & Schuster.

and out of high school. By age thirty-five, he was doing well in his career, but no one was predicting great accomplishments. As a staff officer in a large, European-based manufacturing firm, he had a good but not great reputation. When I interviewed him in

1982, the word *leader* never occurred to me. A dozen years later, the story had changed greatly.

By 1994, Marcel was the head of his own company, had hundreds of employees, and was very wealthy. He had invented a product and a market and had built an organization to capitalize on both. Within his world, he was known as a "visionary." One person with whom I talked went on and on about Marcel's "charisma." All this from a guy that didn't much impress me in 1982.

In attempting to explain Marcel's success, I think we are all inclined to look for lucky breaks, and good fortune certainly can be found in his case. But one can also see a difficult business environment that served up plenty of bad luck and hardship. What is striking about Marcel's story is how the bad times didn't wear him down but instead served as a source of learning and growth.

When hit with an unexpected downturn, he would often become angry or morose, but he would never give up or let defensiveness paralyze him. He reflected on good times and bad, and tried to learn from both. Confronting his mistakes, he minimized the arrogant attitudes that often accompany success. With a relatively humble view of himself, he watched more closely and listened more carefully than did most others. As he learned, he relentlessly tested new ideas, even if that meant pushing himself out of his zone of comfort or taking some personal risks.

Listening with an open mind, trying new things, reflecting honestly on successes and failures—none of this requires a high IQ, an MBA degree, or a privileged background. Yet remarkably few people behave in these ways today, especially after age thirty-five and especially when they are already doing well in their careers. But by using these relatively simple techniques, Marcel, Manny, Matsushita, and people like them keep growing while others level off or decline. As a result, they become more and more comfortable with change, they actualize whatever leadership potential they possess, and they help their firms adapt to a rapidly shifting global economy.

THE POWER OF COMPOUNDED GROWTH

If you study the Marcels, Mannys, and Matsushitas of the world, you find that the secret to their capacity to develop leadership and other skills is closely related to the power of compounded growth.

Consider this simple example. Between age thirty and fifty, Fran "grows" at the rate of 6 percent—that is, every year she expands her career-relevant skills and knowledge by 6 percent. Her twin sister, Janice, has exactly the same intelligence, skills, and information at age thirty, but during the next twenty years she grows at only 1 percent per year. Perhaps Janice becomes smug and complacent after early successes. Or maybe Fran has some experience that sets a fire underneath her. The question here is, how much difference will this relatively small learning differential make by age fifty?

Given the facts about Fran and Janice, it's clear that the former will be able to do more at age fifty than the latter. But most of us underestimate how much more capable Fran will become. The confusion surrounds the effect of compounding. Just as we often don't realize the difference over twenty years between a bank account earning 7 percent versus 4 percent, we regularly underestimate the effects of learning differentials.

For Fran and Janice, the difference between a 6 percent and a 1 percent growth rate over twenty years is huge. If they each have 100 units of career-related capability at age thirty, twenty years later, Janice will have 122 units, while Fran will have 321. Peers at age thirty, the two will be in totally different leagues at age fifty.

If the world of the twenty-first century were going to be stable, regulated, and prosperous, sort of like the 1950s and 1960s in the United States, then differential growth rates would be of only modest relevance. In that world, while Fran would likely be considered more accomplished than her sister, both would do just fine. Stability, regulation, and prosperity would reduce competition along with the need for growth, leadership skills, and transformation. But that's not what the future holds.

Just as organizations are going to be forced to learn, change, and constantly reinvent themselves in the twenty-first century, so will increasing numbers of individuals. Lifelong learning and the leadership skills that can be developed through it were relevant to only a small percentage of the population until recently. That percentage will undoubtedly grow over the next few decades.

HABITS OF THE LIFELONG LEARNER

So how do the Frans and Mannys do it? Not with rocket science. The habits they develop are relatively simple (as summarized in exhibit 2 on the facing page).

Lifelong learners take risks. Much more than others, these men and women push themselves out of their comfort zones and try new ideas. While most of us become set in our ways, they keep experimenting.

Risk taking inevitably produces both bigger successes and bigger failures. Much more than most of us, lifelong learners humbly and honestly reflect on their experiences to educate themselves. They don't sweep failure under the rug or examine it from a defensive position that undermines their ability to make rational conclusions.

Lifelong learners actively solicit opinions and ideas from others. They don't make the assumption that they know it all or that most other people have little to contribute. Just the opposite, they believe that with the right approach, they can learn from anyone under almost any circumstance.

Much more than the average person, lifelong learners also listen carefully, and they do so with an open mind. They don't assume that listening will produce big ideas or important information very often. Quite the contrary. But they know that careful listening will help give them accurate feedback on the effect of their actions. And without honest feedback, learning becomes almost impossible.

EXHIBIT 2
Mental Habits That Support Lifelong Learning

➤ *Risk taking:* Willingness to push oneself out of comfort zones

➤ *Humble self-reflection:* Honest assessment of successes and failures, especially the latter

➤ *Solicitation of opinions:* Aggressive collection of information and ideas from others

➤ *Careful listening:* Propensity to listen to others

➤ *Openness to new ideas:* Willingness to view life with an open mind

Q: But these habits are so simple. Why don't more of us develop them?

A: Because in the short term, it's more painful.

Risk taking brings failure as well as success. Honest reflection, listening, solicitation of opinions, and openness bring bad news and negative feedback as well as interesting ideas. In the short term, life is generally more pleasant without failure and negative feedback.

Lifelong learners overcome a natural human tendency to shy away from or abandon habits that produce short-term pain. By surviving difficult experiences, they build up a certain immunity to hardship. With clarity of thought, they come to realize the importance of both these habits and lifelong learning. But most of all, their goals and aspirations facilitate the development of humility, openness, willingness to take risks, and the capacity to listen.

The very best lifelong learners and leaders I've known seem to have high standards, ambitious goals, and a real sense of mission in their lives. Such goals and aspirations spur them on, put their accomplishments in a humbling perspective, and help them endure the short-term pain associated with growth. Sometimes this sense of mission is developed early in life, sometimes later in adulthood, often a combination of the two. Whatever the case, their aspirations help keep them from sliding into a comfortable, safe routine characterized by little sensible risk taking, a relatively closed mind, a minimum of reaching out, and little listening.

Just as a challenging vision can help an organization to adapt to shifting conditions, nothing seems to support the habits that promote personal growth more than ambitious, humanistic goals.

Twenty-first-Century Careers

The more volatile economic environment, along with the need for more leadership and lifelong learning, is also producing careers that look quite different from those typical of the twentieth century.

Most of the successful white-collar workers in the past hundred years found reputable companies to work for early in their lives and then moved up narrow functional hierarchies while learning the art of management. Most successful blue-collar workers found companies with good unions, learned how to do a certain job, and then stayed in that position for decades. In the twenty-first century, neither of these career paths will provide many people with a good life because neither encourages sufficient lifelong learning, especially for leadership skills.

The problem for the blue-collar worker is more obvious. Union rules have often discouraged personal growth. Narrow job classifications, for example, weren't designed to reduce learning, but that has been one of the consequences. In a stable environment, we could live with those kinds of rules. In a rapidly changing globalized marketplace, we probably cannot.

The old white-collar career path did help people learn, but only in narrow functional grooves. One had to absorb more and more knowledge about accounting (or engineering or marketing), but little else. To progress beyond a certain level, one had to learn about management, but not much about leadership.

Successful twenty-first-century careers will be more dynamic. Already we are seeing less linear movement up a single hierarchy. Already we are seeing fewer people doing one job the same way for long periods of time. The greater uncertainty and volatility tend to be uncomfortable for people at first. But most of us seem to get used to it. And the benefits can certainly be significant.

People who learn to master more volatile career paths also usually become more comfortable with change generally and thus better able to play more useful roles in organizational transformations. They more easily develop whatever leadership potential they have. With more leadership, they are in a better position to help their employers advance the transformation process so as to significantly improve meaningful results while minimizing the painful effects of change.

That Necessary Leap into the Future

For a lot of reasons, many people are still embracing the twentieth-century career and growth model. Sometimes complacency is the problem. They have been successful, so why change? Sometimes they have no clear vision of the twenty-first century, and so they don't know how they should change. But often fear is a key issue. They see jobs seeming to disappear all around them. They hear horror stories about people who have been downsized or reengineered out of work. They worry about health insurance and the cost of college for their children. So they don't think about growth. They don't think about personal renewal. They don't think about developing whatever leadership potential they have. Instead they cling defensively to what they currently have. In effect, they embrace the past, not the future.

A strategy of embracing the past will probably become increasingly ineffective over the next few decades. Better for most of us to start learning now how to cope with change, to develop whatever leadership potential we have, and to help our organizations in the transformation process. Better for most of us, despite the risks, to leap into the future. And to do so sooner rather than later.

As an observer of life in organizations, I think I can say with some authority that people who are making an effort to embrace the future are a happier lot than those who are clinging to the past. That is not to say that learning how to become a part of the twenty-first-century enterprise is easy. But people who are attempting to grow, to become more comfortable with change, to develop leadership skills—these men and women are typically driven by a sense that they are doing what is right for themselves, their families, and their organizations. That sense of purpose spurs them on and inspires them during rough periods.

And those people at the top of enterprises today who encourage others to leap into the future, who help them overcome natural fears, and who thus expand the leadership capacity in their organizations—these people provide a profoundly important service for the entire human community.

We need more of those people. And we will get them.

Photo: Richard Chase

About the Author

John P. Kotter is the Konosuke Matsushita Professor of Leadership at the Harvard Business School and the founder and a principal of Kotter Associates in Cambridge, Massachusetts. A graduate of MIT and Harvard, he has been on the Harvard Business School faculty since 1972. In 1980, at the age of thirty-three, he was given tenure and a full professorship at the school, making him one of the youngest people in Harvard's history to be so honored.

Professor Kotter is the author of *The General Managers* (1982), *Power and Influence: Beyond Formal Authority* (1985), *The Leadership Factor* (1987), *A Force for Change: How Leadership Differs from Management* (1990), *Corporate Culture and Performance* (with James L. Heskett, 1992), and *The New Rules: How to Succeed in Today's Post-Corporate World* (1995), all bestsellers among business books in the United States. He has also created two highly acclaimed executive videos, *Leadership* (1991) and *Corporate Culture* (1993). His articles in the *Harvard Business Review* over the past twenty years have sold well over a million reprints.

The many honors won by Professor Kotter include an Exxon Award for Innovation in Graduate Business School Curriculum Design; a Johnson, Smith & Knisely Award for New Perspectives in Business Leadership; and a McKinsey Award for best *Harvard Business Review* article.

Professor Kotter is a frequent speaker at top management meetings around the world. He lives in Cambridge, Massachusetts, and at Squam Lake, New Hampshire, with his wife, Nancy, and children, Caroline and Jonathan.